A Practical Guide for Raising a Self-Directed and Caring Child

An Alternative to the Tiger Mother Parenting Style

A Practical Guide for Raising a Self-Directed and Caring Child

*An Alternative to the Tiger
Mother Parenting Style*

Louis J. Lichtman, PhD

iUniverse, Inc.
Bloomington

A Practical Guide for Raising a Self-Directed and Caring Child
An Alternative to the Tiger Mother Parenting Style

iUniverse books may be ordered through booksellers or by contacting:

iUniverse
1663 Liberty Drive
Bloomington, IN 47403
www.iuniverse.com
1-800-Authors (1-800-288-4677)

Because of the dynamic nature of the Internet, any web addresses or links contained in this book may have changed since publication and may no longer be valid. The views expressed in this work are solely those of the author and do not necessarily reflect the views of the publisher, and the publisher hereby disclaims any responsibility for them.

Any people depicted in stock imagery provided by Thinkstock are models, and such images are being used for illustrative purposes only.

Certain stock imagery © Thinkstock.

ISBN: 978-1-4502-9361-7 (sc)
ISBN: 978-1-4502-9362-4 (ebook)
ISBN: 978-1-4502-9363-1 (hc)

Library of Congress Control Number: 2011905767

Printed in the United States of America

iUniverse rev. date: 4/26/2011

CONTENTS

PREFACE

I became an assistant professor of psychology at Alfred University in 1970. In 1987, a graduate-level psychology course I usually taught every fall semester got delayed one semester, providing me with an opportunity to introduce a new course that I incorrectly anticipated would be a one-time-only offering. At the time I was deciding what new course I would teach, my life was quite hectic. Each weekday from early in the morning until 12:45 in the afternoon, I was taking care of Andrea, my younger daughter, who at the time was two years old; in the afternoons and evenings, I was teaching a full load of courses. I was also using a large portion of each weekend to prepare lectures and grade exams and papers. In addition, I was the person who had primary responsibility for the operation of a Montessori preschool I helped to found four years earlier.

I debated between introducing a new course in health psychology, which closely related to other things I taught and would have been a relatively easy new preparation for me, or a new course on parenting, which was an entirely new type of course for me and would require a great deal of preparation. Because I was so very busy, I was heavily leaning toward taking the easy way out and going with the health psychology course, but a phone call changed all that. One night while I was preparing dinner and taking care of Andrea and my older daughter Karen, who at the time was six, the phone rang and a woman at the other end asked if I would participate in a phone survey. I said I would, but only if it would take no more than ten minutes, because I had to finish cooking dinner and then rush off to teach a class. The woman assured me that ten minutes would be sufficient.

The survey involved a series of questions about major events taking place in the world, each followed by a set of answers to select from. After ten minutes had expired, I told the woman that I couldn't afford the time to continue, but she begged me, saying that there were only two survey questions left. I continued, and the last question on the survey changed the course of my academic life. That question was, "What do you think is the most significant problem facing our country today?" While I don't remember the exact answer choices she gave, I do remember that they included obvious things, such as the high crime rate, the poor economy, racial tensions, and the destruction of the environment. Each set of answers I was given to select from also included the option to choose "other," meaning none of the above. I thought for some time and then chose "other" as my answer. I could tell from the tone of the woman's voice that the choice of "other" as an answer to this particular question was a most unusual one. She then said that if I wanted to share with her what I thought was the most significant problem facing our country today, she had a place on the survey form to include my response. I answered, "Parenting—I believe the way children are being raised today is the most serious problem facing our nation." Upon hanging up the phone, I immediately knew that although it would take a considerable amount of preparation, if I felt that strongly, I really had no choice but to offer a parenting course in the fall.

At that time, my concern about the way children were being raised largely stemmed from contact I had had with a considerable number of unhappy and poorly adjusted college students, many of whom appeared to me to have good reason to be upset with the way they had been raised. Another contributing factor was the contact I had had during the previous four years with parents of children enrolled in the Montessori preschool. My experiences since then have led me to feel even more strongly that the lack of quality parenting is indeed the most significant problem facing our nation today. I believe that it is a key factor in many of our societal problems, including the elevated high school dropout rate, drug and alcohol abuse, the high crime rate, the lack of respect for our environment, racism, sexism, ageism, the high divorce rate, the high rate of out-of-wedlock births, and even the poor shape of our economy (because of greed and the inability of many people to delay gratification).

In the fall of 1987, I offered Alfred University's first parenting course. It was taught as a seminar and enrolled fourteen psychology students. We read and discussed four paperback books. I thoroughly enjoyed teaching the course, and most importantly thought that the students learned a lot from taking it. At the end of the semester, the course evaluations that the students completed indicated that I was correct—they had found the course to be extremely valuable, and many recommended that it be made a permanent psychology-department offering. Several even came to my office to try to convince me to alter the normal selection of courses I taught in order to make this course part of my regular teaching load. What convinced me to do so were a couple of students who not only insisted that this course should be made a regular offering, but strongly believed that it should also be a graduation requirement for all university students, regardless of their choice of major. Since 1987, I have taught the parenting seminar course over eighty times. One of the wonderful things about the course is that it very quickly began to attract students from throughout the entire university, which enhanced the experiences and ideas shared in class discussions.

The course mainly enrolls students who are not yet parents, although quite a few students who are parents and even a few who are grandparents have taken it. The primary goal of the course is to help students develop their own set of guiding principles or philosophies of parenting. This book is an outgrowth of that course, and in part reflects my own philosophy of parenting, a philosophy that grew out of personal experience, a reading of parenting literature, and thousands of hours of class discussion.

As the title of the book suggests, two things that I consider to be most important are helping children to become self-directed and caring. In part, I chose to focus on these two things because I think they are often lacking in today's youth, and because without them I think it is very difficult to be successful and to achieve happiness. Also, the era in which we are now living seems to stress personal gain and corporate greed at the expense of caring about people and the environment.

For about the past ten years, people working in educational institutions have adopted the term "helicopter parents" to describe parents who are always hovering overhead in order to monitor and manage their children's lives. The technological innovation that has largely enabled this is the cell phone, which has been called "the world's longest umbilical cord."[1] With the recent publication of Amy Chua's bestselling book the *Battle Hymn of the Tiger Mother*, there are many who have come to believe that children will be more successful if they are parent-controlled rather than if they are self-directed. Parents often struggle with letting go of control because they don't have confidence in their children's ability to direct their own lives. However, research has shown that an authoritarian parenting style, where parents control most aspects of a child's life, is not nearly as effective as an authoritative parenting style, where parents encourage children to become self-directed.

A study published in 2010 confirmed my observation that college students are becoming more self-centered and less caring. Between 1979 and 2009, researchers found about a 40 percent decrease in empathetic concern, with the sharpest decline occurring since the year 2000.[2] Compared to college students of the late 1970s, the study reported, today's college students are less likely to agree with statements like "I sometimes try to understand my friends better by imagining how things look from their perspective" and "I often have tender, concerned feelings for people less fortunate than me." Reasons suggested for the decline in empathy include numbing of people to the pain of others resulting from increased exposure to violence in the media, and "the ease of having 'friends' online might make people more likely to just tune out when they don't feel like responding to others' problems, a behavior that could carry over offline."[3] However, I personally believe that parenting is a contributing factor.

While this book is largely based on research findings, it is written as a practical guide. It carefully explains what parents can do if they want to raise children who are self-directed and caring. It begins with a discussion of what an individual should consider before deciding to become a parent and how to give children the best possible start in life. It then focuses on how to build a child's self-esteem and how parenting styles and discipline practices influence a child's behavior and character. Special attention is also given to the topics of achievement, parenting during the adolescent years, and the way family structure impacts children. The book ends with a discussion of how to avoid twelve common mistakes parents make.

CHAPTER 1
GETTING READY TO BECOME A PARENT

- What kinds of things should you think about in advance of becoming a parent?
  a. Do you really want to become a parent?
  b. Are you ready for the awesome responsibility involved in raising a child?
  c. Are you able to provide the time and material resources that a child requires?
  d. How does having a child impact marital/couple satisfaction and lifestyle?
  e. What parenting style would you like to use to raise your future child?
  f. What qualities and characteristics would you like to help your future child develop?
- How can financial planning in advance of having children reduce stress and increase options?
- Why is it helpful to understand that parenting is a very difficult and ever-changing job?
  a. Image-Making Stage
  b. Nurturing Stage
  c. Authority Stage
  d. Interpretative Stage
  e. Interdependent Stage
  f. Departure Stage

- How has the nature of parenting dramatically changed in recent decades?
- What emotions are experienced when a couple learns they are going to become parents?

WHAT KINDS OF THINGS SHOULD YOU THINK ABOUT IN ADVANCE OF BECOMING A PARENT?

Do you really want to become a parent?

Because society puts tremendous pressure on people to marry and have children, many married couples and couples in long-term relationships automatically assume that they will eventually have children, without ever giving serious thought as to whether they really want to become parents. As a result, they rarely seriously consider the advantages and disadvantages of becoming parents or staying childless. This is unfortunate.

In an ideal world, two people who are in love with each other and who have been in a long-term stable relationship would spend a considerable amount of time talking about how they feel about children and their views on child-rearing *before* deciding if parenting children together should be a part of their future. This is because couples who have serious discussions about children and child-rearing before becoming parents are better prepared to be parents, and tend to be happier and more successful parents.[1, 2]

Through discussions of this type, sometimes couples learn that they have drastically different views about children and child-rearing and decide to stay together but not have children, or to separate and seek out new relationships with others whose views more closely match theirs. This is wise, since it is best to coparent children with a person who generally shares your views on children and parenting.

Parents who seriously disagree about how to raise their children experience considerable stress and unhappiness, tend to be inconsistent in their parenting practices, and tend to have a less stable relationship, all of which isn't good for them or for their children.[3] Because most parents consider their children to be the single most important part of their lives, the importance of having a coparent with compatible views can't be over-emphasized. It clearly makes parenting, a stressful activity under the best of circumstances, much less stressful and much more likely to have a successful outcome.

Of course, we don't live in an ideal world. Many people have children without ever having given serious thought to what parenting is all about and how having children will change their lives. This, in part, is because about 50 percent of pregnancies are unplanned, so many people learn that they are going to be parents long before they have given much thought to what it might be like to be a parent or to coparent together.[4] Also, for a variety of reasons including separation, divorce, and death of a partner, many people who do not want to be single parents become single parents for at least part of the time they are raising children, and they and their children miss the potential benefits that coparenting can provide.

Whether you are in an ideal or less-than-ideal situation, if children will soon become part of your life, it is important to give some serious thought to the kind of parent you would like to become. If you have a partner with whom you are going to coparent, the two of you should be formulating and sharing your views on parenting. By doing this, you will likely find that a common approach to the more fundamental aspects of raising children will emerge.

For those who are already parents but have not yet given serious thought to the kind of parent they would really like to be, it's not too late. Begin now, either alone or with a coparent, to evaluate how you function as a parent and how you would like to function in the future. This kind of analysis can help to motivate you to make positive changes in how you approach parenting.

Whether you will soon be a parent or are already one, if you are not knowledgeable about different styles of parenting and normal child development, take the time to learn by reading books, attending workshops, or taking courses. Doing so will help you to become a better parent.

Are you ready for the awesome responsibility involved in raising a child?

Most people view parenting as one of the most important responsibilities that a person can have, yet unlike many other important responsibilities, most people receive little formal education or preparation to undertake this responsibility. Think about all of the formal training and/or education that is typically required to master a new job or prepare for a career, compared to the lack of formal training and education available to learn how to become an effective parent. Also, other important responsibilities are to some degree voluntary, but the responsibility of parenting should never be viewed as such. Many people feel a great deal of responsibility toward their work, but they do have the option of changing jobs or careers, or selling a business that they may own. Most people feel a responsibility to their marriage, but they do have the option of getting a separation or a divorce. Children, on the other hand, should be viewed as a lifelong responsibility. Parents should always be there for their children, regardless of age. If you are thinking about having a child, you should ask yourself if you are ready to take on this awesome responsibility.

Are you able to provide the time and material resources that a child requires?

Typically, a great deal of freedom is lost when one becomes a parent. All responsible parents put the needs of their children first. Doing so requires an investment of both time and money. For one thing, a lot of time must be devoted to earning money to support a child. According to a US Department of Agriculture (USDA) report, the cost of raising a child from birth to age seventeen (born in 2008 into a two-parent family that already had one child) is estimated (in 2008 dollars) to be $159,870 for families with a before-tax income of less than $56,870; $221,190 for parents earning between $56,870 and $98,470; and $366,600 for those earning more than $98,470.[5] These totals do not include the cost of prenatal care, the cost of giving birth, and the cost of post-secondary education. That means, depending on income level, it costs an average of between $783 and $1,797 per month to raise a second child to age seventeen!

More importantly, parents need to spend a great deal of time and energy interacting with their children. Newborns are almost totally dependent upon their parents for everything. Parents who are sensitive and responsive to their newborns usually establish a close bond, which psychologists call a *secure attachment*. This is important, because in the years ahead, a securely attached child is more likely to be successful than a child who doesn't form a secure attachment (see chapter two, "Giving Children the Best Possible Start," for a discussion of attachment). As the child grows older, responsible parents spend a great deal of time teaching the child all kinds of things about the world they live in. As the years continue to pass, most parents function as chauffeurs, nurses, coaches, cheerleaders, tutors, and so on. By the time a child becomes an adolescent, parents should have invested the time and energy needed to help the child establish a sound set of values and morals. Doing all of this is obviously a lot of hard work, but nurturing the development of a child can also provide a tremendous amount of gratification. If you are thinking of having a child, you should ask yourself if you are ready to invest the time and resources needed to support your child's development. You should also ask yourself if you are ready to put on hold some things that you have wanted to do that take time and money, such as travel plans.

How does having a child impact marital/couple satisfaction and lifestyle?

Many couples are surprised by the way their relationship changes once a child enters the picture. Most childless couples are relatively carefree and devote a tremendous amount of time to each other. After a child is born, the weight of the awesome responsibility quickly begins to be felt, and now the majority of time is typically devoted to the child or to earning money needed to provide resources for the child, and the parents spend much less time alone together. They also frequently find that when they are alone together, their discussions often relate in some way to their child. When the child takes over as the center of attention, it isn't unusual for one parent, usually the father, to become jealous of the amount of time that the other is investing in the child. Once a child enters the picture, going out for an evening or away for a weekend needs to be carefully planned, and the previous pre-child carefree existence will likely be missed.

In addition to having an increased workload and much reduced time for each other, couples often find that once a child arrives, there is a tendency to adopt more traditional gender roles. Childless couples tend to share household tasks more equally.[6] Following the birth of a child, fathers tend to focus more on being the breadwinner, and mothers tend to focus more on taking care of the home and the newborn baby. This is due in part to that fact that mothers tend to be more comfortable around babies, since while growing up they typically spent more time caring for young children than fathers did. Also, because of the gender wage gap, males tend to have greater earning power, and hence the family will likely financially benefit more if the father increases his working hours than if the mother increases hers. Gender-role modification results in resentment only if one person begins to feel that he or she is carrying more than a fair share of the total workload, or if either person would prefer to trade places/roles with the partner.

The combination of additional workload, gender-role modification and possible role conflict, reduced time alone together, reduced sleep time, and decreased sexual activity tends to increase the couple's stress level and helps to explain why the level of marital/couple satisfaction often decreases when a child enters the picture.[7] The more children a couple has, the lower the couple's satisfaction level tends to be. According to a report in the *Journal of Family Psychiatry*, "Most prenatal classes prioritize the physical aspects of labor and delivery, and fail to incorporate the social and emotional changes and stressors that new parents often experience—prenatal classes might be expanded to incorporate sessions focused on other aspects of becoming a parent, as well as encouraging communication between partners regarding their expectations of parenthood."[8]

Of course, the more stable the couple's relationship before having a child, the easier it is to cope with all of the changes. Despite the increased stress level, having children also has the potential to bring couples closer together, since they now share an important common focus. If you are thinking about becoming a parent, you should ask yourself if you are ready to cope with the relationship and lifestyle changes that are bound to come with having a child.

What parenting style would you like to use to raise your future child?

In thinking ahead about the type of parent you would like to become, one of the most important things to consider is parenting style. Do you want to be a strict/restrictive parent who has rigid rules and administers serious consequences for rule violations? Do you want to have flexible rules that you will adjust in special circumstances and that you will allow your child to challenge? Do you want to be a lenient/permissive/indulgent parent who has few rules, buys your child whatever he/she wants, and functions much like a friend to your child?

Do you want to be the kind of parent who knows what is best for your child and makes decisions for your child based on that knowledge, or do you prefer to be the kind of parent who guides and then steps aside to let your child make his/her own decisions? Do you want to be the type of parent who explains the reasons for the rules that you have put in place as well as the decisions you make, or do you want to be the kind of parent who simply says "Because I said so." Perhaps you would like to draw from several of these parenting styles and create your own unique parenting style. You should give some serious thought to the style of parenting you want to use as the foundation for the child-rearing decisions you will constantly be making once you are a parent. Chapter four, "Discipline and Parenting Styles," includes a thorough discussion of the different parenting styles and the outcomes that are typically associated with each of them.

What qualities and characteristics would you like to help your future child develop?

Some thought should be given to the type of person you would like your child to become. What kinds of qualities and characteristics would you like to help your child develop? Knowing what you hope to accomplish will help you as you go about making day-to-day parenting decisions. The primary focus of this book is to help parents raise children who are self-directed and caring, but there are many other qualities and characteristics that parents might want to stress, such as honesty, cooperation, ambition, spirituality, and friendliness.

How can financial planning in advance of having children reduce stress and increase options?

As pointed out earlier in this chapter, raising a child is very expensive. Some serious planning is needed in order to be sure that you have the financial resources available to support a child. One of the most common and serious mistakes that future parents make is to be living a lifestyle that requires all or most of their available income. If a couple is using virtually all of their income to meet current expenses, how will they find the extra $800 to $1,800 per month needed to cover the additional expenses associated with raising a child? Most people are unable to scale back enough on their monthly expenses to come up with that much money without making some drastic and stressful changes, such as moving to a much less expensive dwelling or giving up one of their cars. Considering the financial realities of having a child and the fact that arguing over money, more than arguing over anything else, is the best predictor of divorce, financial planning should be made a top priority.[9] A 2010 survey found that only about a quarter of couples talk about finances and work out a budget before getting married.[10]

If a couple is planning on having a child, it makes sense for them to be living a lifestyle that only requires two-thirds to three-quarters of their current income, and to save the rest. Doing this for a few years will allow a nice nest egg to accumulate. A small portion of the nest egg could be used to help cover the cost of getting things ready for the child, including buying a crib and other furniture and equipment. Once the child arrives, the portion of income that had previously been saved should be enough to cover the additional monthly expenses. The rest of the nest egg opens up options, such as enabling the mother to take an unpaid leave if there are pregnancy complications or enabling one parent to take a large block of time off from work to be home with the newborn. The nest egg could also help provide the funds needed to support any additional children that the couple may have.

WHY IS IT HELPFUL TO UNDERSTAND THAT PARENTING IS A VERY DIFFICULT AND EVER-CHANGING JOB?

Helping a newborn develop into a happy and productive adult is a task that requires a constantly changing set of skills. Just think about the concerns that a parent of a newborn faces compared to the concerns that the parent of a teenager faces. Ellen Galinsky, an author of parenting books and parenting expert for Lifetime Television, outlined six different stages of parenting.[11] For each stage, she described different issues and challenges typically faced by parents. Having an idea of what is involved in navigating the six stages is of value to every parent, and to every prospective parent.

Image-Making Stage

During pregnancy, the major task is to prepare for childbirth and parenthood. The future parents begin to imagine what their child might be like and how they will function as parents. As they start to think about the awesome responsibility that lies ahead, they will likely begin to realize that their lives are about to dramatically change. It is common for the prospective parents to experience some fear and trepidation, since there is much uncertainty in what lies ahead.

Nurturing Stage

During infancy, the major challenge facing parents is to help the child to become securely attached to them. To accomplish this, parents need to be sensitive and responsive to their child. This includes knowing when the child is becoming upset and trying to comfort the child, being tuned in on signs that indicate that the child is hungry and feeding the child, and observing sounds and movements that the child makes and reacting to them. Spending time holding, cuddling, hugging, rocking, and talking to the child also helps with the attachment process.

Authority Stage

During the preschool years, parents need to establish rules. A great deal of communication between parents usually takes place during this stage in order to decide on what the rules will be and how they will be enforced. Ideally, there should also be a lot of communication occurring between the parents and the child to help the child fully understand the reasons for the rules.

Interpretive Stage

During the elementary-school years, parents typically spend a great deal of time teaching the child about life and explaining how the world works. This typically involves answering innumerable questions so the child can gain knowledge, develop skills, and begin to establish values. In the process of doing all of this teaching, parents often refine their own beliefs.

Interdependent Stage

During the adolescent years, children often struggle with identity issues. They strive to figure out just who they are, how they stack up against others, and who they would someday like to become. At the same time, they are working toward establishing their independence. They want to make their own decisions and run their own lives. Parents often have trouble relinquishing control, usually because they still feel responsible for their child and may think that their child isn't yet capable of functioning well without their guidance. Often a power struggle develops and, as a result, this can be a very stressful time for the entire family.

Departure Stage

As children become young adults, they typically wish to strike out on their own. After so many years of being child-focused, parents now need to let go. They need to pull back from trying to mold their child and accept their child for the person he/she has become. They often also need to redefine themselves, since the role of parent should now consume a lot less of their time.

During the process of helping a child develop into an adult, clearly very different types of demands are placed on parents and different skill sets are called upon. One of the biggest disadvantages of being a single parent is the lack of a partner with whom to share all of this. While every parent should be involved in all stages, clearly having a partner allows one parent to take the lead role during some stages and the other the lead role during other stages. In cases where part of the extended family lives together or nearby, grandparents, uncles and aunts, and other relatives may be able to assist with meeting some of the ever-changing demands placed on parents.

How has the nature of parenting dramatically changed in recent decades?

Not that long ago, the vast majority of mothers stayed at home to raise their children. Because today there are a large number of dual-career couples, as well as a large number of single-parent families, that arrangement is a lot less common. In 2008, 59.6 percent of mothers of married-couple families with children under the age of six were employed, and 64.4 percent of mothers in mother-maintained single-parent families were employed.[12]

When the norm was for mothers to stay at home and raise children, the opportunities for women (and to some degree for men) were clearly restricted. However, that arrangement did provide some clear advantages for children as well as some disadvantages. One major advantage was having a parent whose primary responsibility was taking care of the children. Today, most parents are employed and hence have at least two primary responsibilities, their children and their work. This means that they have considerably less time and energy to devote to their children. In 2008, full-time employed married woman with children under the age of six spent an average of 1.6 hours per weekday doing primary child care, while unemployed married women with children under the age of six spent almost double that amount of time doing primary child care (3.4 hours per weekday).[13] Primary child care was defined as physical care of children; playing, reading, or talking with children; travel related to child care; and other child-care activities. A major concern of employed parents is finding a good child-care arrangement, a topic that is covered in chapter two, "Giving Children the Best Possible Start."

One potential disadvantage of children being raised by stay-at-home mothers is the children not realizing the full potential of women. It is likely that children raised in this manner will come to view both capabilities and opportunities along narrow gender lines. Another disadvantage of not having a working mother is that the family will have less income.

Another major, relatively recent societal change that impacts children is the high divorce rate and high rate of births to unwed parents. Unfortunately, the combination of these two factors has resulted in many children growing up without the presence of one parent in the home, usually the father. Children often experience this as a type of parental abandonment, a topic discussed in chapter five, "Divorce and Family Configurations."

Because most homes have TV and the Internet, it is now no longer possible to protect children from being exposed to things that they are not developmentally ready to understand. For example, when my oldest daughter was three years old, she asked me what the word "rape" meant. I had been watching the nightly news, and there was a report on a rape case that she overheard. Ideally, it would be best to discuss a topic like rape when children are older, but in today's world we no longer have that option. Since we can no longer protect children from exposure to such topics, we are often forced to discuss them at a less-than-ideal time in their development.

The world today is a lot less safe for children than it used to be. Not too long ago, people were less mobile and got to know their neighbors well. Most parents used to be comfortable with letting children go outside to play with their friends. They knew that their neighbors (especially during the time of stay-at-home mothers) would be there to provide some guidance or supervision should their children require it. In today's mobile society, people often don't know their neighbors, and parents are reluctant to allow their children to play outside unsupervised. This means that children are spending a lot more time inside, often interacting with electronic devices, and a lot less time exploring their neighborhoods and playing with their friends. This slows the development of their independence and self-reliance. It also reduces physical activity, one of the reasons for today's childhood obesity epidemic.

WHAT EMOTIONS ARE EXPERIENCED WHEN A COUPLE LEARNS THEY ARE GOING TO BECOME PARENTS?

The initial emotions felt by expectant parents in part depend upon whether the pregnancy was planned or unplanned. If the pregnancy was planned and there is knowledge or expectation that the developing fetus is healthy, typically a tremendous amount of joy and excitement will be experienced as well as some fear and anxiety, since the couple will likely begin to second-guess whether they are really ready to handle all that parenting entails. There may also be some concern about pain involved in delivery and possible birth complications. If an expectant couple learns that their developing child has problems, guilt is a commonly experienced emotion. They will likely wonder if in some way they might be responsible for the problems. If it took a long time for the planned pregnancy to take place, a wonderful feeling of relief will also be experienced if no problems are anticipated.

If the pregnancy is unplanned, a wider range of emotions may be experienced, including surprise, excitement, joy, fear, anger, disappointment, panic, and sadness. Which of these emotions are experienced will of course depend on many factors, including the nature of the relationship of the parents-to-be, whether part of their plans included someday having children together, and whether they decide to raise the child themselves, give it up for adoption, or have an abortion.

Whether or not the pregnancy was planned, there may be some concern about how the couple's relationship will change when they actually become parents.

SUMMARY

Many people become parents without having first given serious thought to what is involved in raising a child and how having a child will change their lives. This is unfortunate, since people are happier and more successful as parents if they have discussions about children and parenting in advance of becoming parents. Ideally, discussions should take place about the awesome responsibility that parenting entails, the time and material resources that children require, the parenting style to be employed, and how having a child is likely to impact marital/couple satisfaction. It is also helpful for parents and future parents to understand that successfully raising a child takes an ever-changing set of skills.

CHAPTER 2
GIVING CHILDREN THE BEST POSSIBLE START

- Why is good prenatal and early postnatal care, especially good nutrition, extremely important for both mother and developing child?
- How does early stimulation help to build a better brain?
- Why is it important for children to emotionally bond with their parents or caretakers?
- Why is it important for parents to learn about normal child development and techniques of parenting?
- How should parents go about selecting a child-care arrangement?

WHY IS GOOD PRENATAL AND EARLY POSTNATAL CARE, ESPECIALLY GOOD NUTRITION, EXTREMELY IMPORTANT FOR BOTH MOTHER AND DEVELOPING CHILD?

Good nutrition during pregnancy is of crucial importance. According to the National Eating Disorder Association, "During pregnancy, the growing baby receives all its nourishment from the mother's body. When stores of carbohydrates, proteins, fats, vitamins, minerals and other nutrients are low, a woman's body will drain them to support the growth and development of the baby. If reserves are not sufficiently restored through healthy eating, the mother can become severely malnourished, and this in turn can lead to depression, exhaustion, and many other serious health complications."[1] Of course, if the mother's nutritional resources are depleted, there are health consequences for the developing fetus.

When a woman is pregnant and aspects of her eating disorders continue, she may not be able to provide all of the nutrients that her developing child needs, making her less likely to give birth to a healthy baby. The same is true of women who don't suffer from an eating disorder but for other reasons are poorly nourished during pregnancy. Undernourishment in the womb affects fetal growth and increases the chances that women will give birth to low-birth-weight babies (less than 5.5 pounds) whose development is compromised. Poor prenatal and neonatal nutrition are associated with neurological impairment and poorer cognitive functioning, including lower overall intelligence, more learning disabilities, poorer attention skills, and poorer school performance.[2, 3, 4, 5] Undernourishment in the womb also increases the risk that heart disease, diabetes, strokes, and high blood pressure will develop later in life. [6]

For the health of both the expectant mother and her developing child, prenatal vitamin supplements should be taken before and during pregnancy. Folic acid, calcium, and iron are especially important. Insufficient amounts of folic acid (a B-vitamin), can lead to miscarriages and neural tube defects, such as spina bifida, a disorder in which the vertebrae (bones) that surround the spinal cord have not formed properly and components of the spinal cord may protrude.[7] Children with spina bifida often have trouble with movement and sensation in their lower limbs and may have difficulty with bowel or bladder control. If all women, starting at least one month before pregnancy and continuing though the first trimester of pregnancy, were to take an adequate amount of folic acid (current recommendation is 400 micrograms per day before pregnancy and 600 micrograms per day during pregnancy) it is estimated that 75 percent of neural-tube defects would be prevented.[8] Although less common, neural-tube defects can also affect brain development. Calcium is important for the bone growth of the fetus and helps prevent the expectant mother from losing her own bone density. Iron is an important component of hemoglobin, which is the oxygen-carrying component of blood, and iron also plays an important role in brain development. Iron deficiency affects a number of brain regions, including the hippocampus, which is important in memory.[9]

Alcohol consumption during pregnancy can negatively impact the developing fetus. The term fetal alcohol spectrum disorders (FASD) is used to describe the many problems associated with alcohol passing though the placenta and affecting the developing fetus.[10] The most severe form of FASD is fetal alcohol syndrome (FAS), a condition in which babies are born smaller in size, have facial anomalies, and have serious cognitive limitations. They may also suffer from heart, liver, and kidney problems. Although at one time it was believed that an occasional drink during pregnancy would cause no harm, we now know that no level of drinking is totally safe. While FASDs are certainly more likely to occur with frequent and heavy alcohol consumption, even moderate or light drinking can impair development.[11, 12]

Because about 50 percent of pregnancies are unplanned, many women are consuming alcohol at the time of conception and continue to do so until they learn that they are pregnant, which often isn't until a month or two later. Also, some women who are trying to get pregnant continue to consume alcohol but plan to stop consumption once they know that they are pregnant, which again might not be until a month or two after conception. This is a serious problem, because early in pregnancy, alcohol exposure can result in the child being born with a smaller and poorly organized brain. The smaller size is a result of fewer neurons (brain cells important in information transmission) surviving, and the disorganization is a result of abnormal neuron migration (movement of neurons from the area of production to their final destination).[13] Depending on the degree of neural impairment, the child may suffer serious mental retardation or just have a slightly lower IQ. Other cognitive problems associated with fetal alcohol exposure, include attention deficit hyperactivity disorder (ADHD) and learning disabilities (LDs), which include speech and language delays.[14] Considering the potentially serious consequences of exposing a fetus to alcohol, sexually active women of childbearing age who are not using contraception should not consume any alcohol.

Because breastfeeding provides "health, nutritional, immunologic, developmental, psychological, social, economic, and environmental benefits," the American Academy of Pediatrics and many other health organizations recommend exclusive breastfeeding for the first six months of life.[15] Exclusive breastfeeding is defined as an infant's consumption of human milk with no supplementation of any type (no water, no juice, no nonhuman milk, and no foods) except for vitamins, minerals, and medications. Infants who are breastfed receive protection from a wide range of infectious diseases, including bacterial meningitis, respiratory-tract infections, urinary-tract infections, middle-ear infections, and diarrhea. They also experience a reduction in the incidence of both type 1 and type 2 diabetes, leukemia, and asthma, and have lower infant mortality rates.[16] Cognitive benefits of breastfeeding, as measured by IQ test performance and teacher's academic ratings, have also been reported.[17, 18] Adults who were breastfed as infants have been found to have lower blood pressure, lower levels of cholesterol, and a reduced incidence of obesity.[19]

Following childbirth, those women who plan to breastfeed should continue to abstain from alcohol consumption; alcohol gets into breast milk and has been shown to slow the development of infant motor skills, including crawling and walking, and interferes with the duration and quality of infant sleep.[20] Also, on average, infants consume "20% less breast milk during the 3 to 4 hours following their mothers consumption of an alcoholic beverage," according to a study in *Alcohol Research and Health*.[21]

In addition to alcohol, the developing fetus is particularly sensitive to other toxic substances, such as lead. Over time, lead accumulates in the body and can affect many organs, including the heart, kidneys, and brain. It interferes with brain development and can cause serious cognitive problems. As in the case of alcohol, what was once considered a safe level of lead exposure no longer is. Lead exposure is determined by the amount of lead, measured in micrograms (mcg), per volume of blood, measured in deciliters (dl). Before 1970, the Centers for Disease Control (CDC) considered a lead level of less than 60 mcg/dl to be safe. In 1970, the CDC lowered the safe lead level to 40 mcg/dl; in 1978, the level was lowered to 30 mcg/dl; in 1985, it was lowered to 25 mcg/dl; and finally, in 1991, it was lowered to 10 mcg/dl. However, a 2003 article published in the *New England Journal of Medicine* found that even a lead level of 10 mcg/dl is high enough to lower IQ scores in young children by about seven points.[22]

Women who have high blood lead levels during pregnancy have a higher incidence of miscarriage and premature delivery. They also have a greater likelihood of delivering a low-birth-weight baby with developmental delays. Pregnant women who have more moderate blood levels of lead are likely to have children who experience subtle cognitive problems. However, most lead exposure comes after birth, when young children eat paint chips or breathe dust from flaking or peeling layers of lead-based house paint. In 1978, the Consumer Product Safety Commission banned the production of lead-based house paint in the United States, but toys imported from foreign countries continue to be recalled because they contain lead-based paint, and older homes still contain walls that originally were painted with lead-based paint. Children may also develop high levels of lead by drinking water contaminated with lead, often as a result of lead-based plumbing materials.

Physical symptoms of lead toxicity in children include headaches, irritability, anemia, stomach pain, vomiting, weight loss, and kidney damage. Behavioral symptoms include lower IQ scores, impaired language development, learning disabilities, attention problems, and aggressive behavior.[23]

Many things besides poor nutrition, alcohol, and lead negatively impact the developing child. Smoking during pregnancy reduces the amount of oxygen getting to the fetus and exposes the fetus to nicotine. This slows fetal body and brain growth, impairs cognitive development, and increases the chances that the child will develop a variety of respiratory problems including asthma, as well as die as a result of sudden infant death syndrome (SIDS). [24, 25] Similar findings have been reported for infants exposed to secondhand smoke.[26] Women who are exposed to high levels of pesticides or mercury during pregnancy have an increased risk of giving birth to a child with cognitive limitations, including memory, learning, and attention problems.[27, 28] Children who have been exposed to high levels of pesticide, most likely though their consumption of fruits and vegetables that have been sprayed with pesticides, also are more likely to develop ADHD.[29]

While research findings have varied, a 2008 study found that pregnant women who ingest more than 200 milligrams of caffeine per day have a greater risk of miscarriage.[30] According to the American Dietary Association, "A cup of coffee contains about 95 milligrams of caffeine, while a 12 ounce can of caffeinated soda contains about 72 milligrams, and a small chocolate candy bar contains about 10 milligrams of caffeine."[31] It should also be mentioned that many drugs, including over-the-counter drugs, prescription drugs, and illegal drugs, may negatively affect fetal development if taken during pregnancy, sometimes in extremely serious ways.

How does early stimulation help to build a better brain?

Starting in the late 1950s, Mark Rosenzweig began a research program to determine if brain development could be influenced by the environment. He and his colleagues discovered that rats raised in stimulating environments developed bigger and better brains.[32] The rats were housed in multilevel group cages, which were equipped with various toys, including seesaws, swings, and ladders. Also, food placement location was changed periodically, and access to an exercise wheel was provided. Among other things, stimulating environments have been shown to increase brain blood flow, increase the thickness of the cortex (the part of the brain most important in cognitive functions), increase in the number of neurons found in the hippocampus (a part of the brain that plays a key role in memory), increase the number and complexity of synapses (resulting in a more complex brain circuitry), and increase the number of glia cells (which support the activity of neurons).[33] Not surprisingly, rats raised in enriched environments have also been shown to be better learners on a wide variety of tasks. Similar brain changes have been found in other species of animals raised in enriched environments, including monkeys.

A limited number of research studies have been done on the effects of environmental manipulation on the developing human brain. The findings of those studies are consistent with the findings of the animal studies. Several studies have found that providing premature infants with either movement stimulation (gently oscillating waterbeds) or stimulation in the form of gentle massage promotes their development.[34] In addition to improving weight gain, they were found to be more alert, to sleep better, to be less irritable, and to have better physical coordination. A 2009 study found that massage of premature infants increases the rate of maturation of both the brain (measured by brain-wave recordings) and the visual system (measured by visual acuity).[35]

It has also been known for a long time that the development of children raised in impoverished orphanages is impaired. Those raised in orphanages where there is little interaction with staff members show severe delays in cognitive and social/emotional development.[36,37] Also, the more time spent in the impoverished orphanage, the smaller the head size, reflecting a smaller-sized brain. In addition, children who spend time in impoverished orphanages have been found to have reduced activity in many brain regions and a reduced number of connections between cortical regions.

Research with animals showing how environmental stimulation enhances brain development was in part responsible for the development of child-enrichment programs like Head Start. In an attempt to break the poverty cycle, Head Start was initiated in 1965 in part to provide poor children with a stimulating environment and increase their chances of reaching their full neurological potential. A Head Start impact study published in 2010 found a number of short-term cognitive benefits and a few longer-term benefits (functioning at end of first grade). The longer-term cognitive benefits were primarily in the area of language development.[38]

But there is no reason to believe that only poor children will benefit from being raised in a stimulating environment. An international review study published in 2010 reported that the vast majority of recent early education and child-care programs show both short- and long-term cognitive benefits for children from all backgrounds.[39] Another 2010 study reported that high-quality child-care produces cognitive benefits that last at least until age fifteen.[40] We now have fifty years of research offering strong evidence that brains function like muscles—they need to be stimulated if they are to fully develop.

Because different parts of the brain are involved in different types of information processing, a wide variety of different types of enrichment activities are needed in order to stimulate the development of the entire brain. For example, it is well known that spending time reading and talking with children improves their language skills and helps with learning how to read.[41] This type of stimulation likely promotes the development of areas of the brain important in language processing, which are primarily located in the left half of the brain. Exposure of children to music, in particular keyboard lessons, has been shown to promote brain development, especially of the right half of the brain.[42]

Creative parents find ways to enrich all kinds of experiences. For example, when reading a storybook to a young child who has not yet begun to talk, a parent can have the child help turn the pages and point to objects located in pictures, stimulating parts of the brain involved in hand-eye coordination, visual attention/recognition, and language comprehension. A parent can also talk about pictures in a book, or after the child acquires the ability to talk, have the child do so, stimulating parts of the brain that are used in visual recognition and language comprehension/expression. Asking older children to guess what comes next in a story that they have heard before is a good way to stimulate parts of the brain involved in memory. If the story is being read for the first time, the same task can be used to stimulate the part of the child's brain involved in imagination. A parent who takes the time to talk with a child about the story and asks the child questions about the story will be helping the child develop parts of the brain that are involved in organization and language expression/comprehension.

Since "play allows children to use their creativity while developing their imagination, dexterity, and physical, cognitive, and emotional strength," according to a study in *Pediatrics*, it is an excellent way to stimulate brain development.[43] Outdoor play also typically provides a considerable amount of physical exercise, which is not only good for maintaining a healthy body but also supports brain development. There is a growing body of literature that indicates that aerobic exercise promotes brain development and enhances cognitive performance for people of all ages. Exercise increases brain blood flow, alters neurotransmitters (the chemicals that neurons use to communicate with each other), and promotes neurogenesis (an increase in the number of neurons).[44, 45] The opportunity for children to play together provides other benefits as well, such as learning to share, to negotiate, and to work in groups. Finally, play offers parents an excellent opportunity to fully engage with their children.

Environmental enrichment can be used not only to build a better brain, but also to repair a damaged brain and/or limit the effects of brain damage on cognition. A number of animal studies have found that many of the negative effects of prenatal exposure to substances like alcohol and lead, or of oxygen deprivation, can be ameliorated or partially ameliorated by environmental enrichment.[46] Education can be considered a form of enrichment, and it increases what is known as *cognitive reserve*, the ability to function well cognitively following brain damage. The more years of education a person receives, the better they appear to be able to cope with various types of brain changes, including those associated with aging, Alzheimer's disease, strokes, epilepsy, and traumatic brain injury.[47]

While providing a highly varied and stimulating environment can be very beneficial, parents should be cautioned that it is a bad idea to pressure young children to practice activities that they don't appear to be interested in, such as learning letters or responding to flash cards. David Elkind, a recognized expert on early child development, calls pushing children to learn things that they aren't developmentally ready to learn "miseducation." Doing so is often stressful for the child, lowers self-esteem, and can be a turnoff to learning. Parents need to be sure that their efforts are primarily motivated by the child's interests and not by their desire to be able to brag about their child's advanced cognitive abilities. This information should be taken into account when choosing a preschool. Preschools that provide a varied and stimulating environment and let children choose how to spend their time are more developmentally appropriate than preschools that have a fixed schedule where children are required to do different lessons throughout the day. In his book *Miseducation,* Elkind writes, "No authority in the field of child psychology, pediatrics, or child psychiatry advocates the formal instruction, in any domain, of infants and young children. In fact, the weight of solid professional opinion opposes it and advocates providing young children with a rich and stimulating environment that is, at the same time, warm, loving, and supportive of the child's own learning priorities and pacing. It is within this supportive, non-pressured environment that infants and young children acquire a solid sense of security, positive self-esteem, and a long-term enthusiasm for learning."[48]

In thinking about this important topic, two personal stories come to mind. When my older daughter, Karen, was four years old, her new preschool teacher came to me very upset. She told me that Karen was spending far too much time painting pictures and doing other types of artwork and not nearly enough time developing her language skills. She said if this continued, my daughter's language development would likely be stunted. I tried to assure the teacher that during the previous year, Karen had spent a lot of time working with language materials at the preschool, and she was still doing so at home. When I told the teacher that I didn't want her to pressure my daughter into doing activities she wasn't interested in, she told me that I was making a big mistake, and that one day I would be sorry. Interestingly, throughout her entire life, Karen has excelled in language-related courses, earned a perfect score of 800 on the verbal SAT test, and currently is completing a doctoral program in applied linguistics. So it would be hard to imagine that her language abilities were in any way stunted by allowing her to pursue her interest in art.

The second personal story involves my younger daughter, Andrea. I spent about five hours per day taking care of Andrea for a two-year period beginning when she was eight months old. When she was exactly two years and three months of age, Andrea and I went to Karen's elementary school to attend Karen's sixth birthday party. While at the party, Karen's first-grade teacher asked me about the kinds of activities that I did with Andrea when we were at home together. Being a strong proponent of the importance of providing an enriched environment, I mentioned a wide variety of different types of stimulation and activities that I was providing, including the fact that I was teaching her to read. In response, the teacher gave me a questioning look and said, "She's only two years old. Do you mean you are teaching her to recognize the names of some letters?" I tried to explain that for about the past six months, Andrea had shown a very strong interest in language activities and several months ago had mastered letter recognition; now was beginning to learn how to read. Thinking that I must have been exaggerating, the teacher once again gave me a questioning look. She then asked me exactly what I meant by reading. In response, I asked the teacher for some paper and a pencil, and I said that because of the excitement of the first-graders partying, and the fact that Andrea was used to reading words made from large brightly colored plastic letters, I wasn't sure if she would be able to read what I was about to write, but I'd give it a try. Without error, Andrea proceeded to read about ten simple three-letter words ending in "at" that I had written (bat, cat, fat, hat). The teacher quickly apologized for her skepticism and said that "by the time Andrea was ready to start elementary school, I wouldn't be surprised if she was able to read the *New York Times*."

Interestingly, very soon after that incident, Andrea lost almost all interest in reading and moved on to other things, such as learning numbers. That was perfectly fine with me, and I didn't pressure her to continue with her reading and possibly turn her off to learning. Her interest in reading was only rekindled very shortly before she was to start elementary school. As a result, when she started elementary school, her reading ability was only slightly better than it was the day of the party.

Based on decades of research, if we want children to reach their full neurological potential, it is essential to provide a stimulating environment for their exploration. If a child were to become interested in a particular type of activity, such as puzzle-making, he/she should be provided with puzzles of appropriately increasing difficulty, but only for as long as the interest continues.

WHY IS IT IMPORTANT FOR CHILDREN TO EMOTIONALLY BOND WITH THEIR PARENTS OR CARETAKERS?

Forming a close emotional attachment with parents (or caretakers) is of fundamental importance to a child's development. The type of bond that develops is largely dependent on the behavior of the parents. Mary Ainsworth, a Canadian psychologist known for her work on the development of attachment, observed children between the ages of twelve and eighteen months as they responded to a situation in which their mothers left them alone and then returned a short time later.[49] Based on the behavior of the infants, Ainsworth described three major types of attachment: secure attachment, ambivalent-insecure attachment, and avoidant-insecure attachment. A fourth pattern, disorganized/disoriented attachment, was identified later by Mary Main and Judith Solomon.[50]

Warm caring parents who enjoy interacting with their child and who are available and highly responsive to their child's needs are likely to establish a secure attachment. According to Ainsworth, a child who is securely attached tends to exhibit some distress when left alone and is happy and seeks closeness when the parent later returns. Children with this type of attachment tend to feel safe and secure, and use their parent as a secure base from which to explore the world or for coping with stressful events. Keeping in close contact with parents during stressful times of course has survival value. The secure feeling is related to the child's ability to be able to depend on parents to get needs met. When an infant communicates a need, often by crying or making sounds, a quick response follows. Because securely attached children are comfortably exploring their environment, they are able to increase the amount of stimulation that they receive from the environment. About 65 percent of infants in the United States have established a secure attachment. Later in life, securely attached children tend to be curious, enthusiastic, persistent, and enjoy trying new things and tackling problems. They also tend to have a positive sense of self, be more sociable, be more self-reliant, perform better in school, and be more likely to graduate from high school than children who do not form a secure attachment[51, 52, 53, 54]

Children of neglectful parents who are not sensitive or responsive to the child's needs are likely to form an anxious-avoidant attachment. They don't show much emotion when a parent leaves and pay little attention or sometimes even avoid that parent when he/she later returns. Their reactions to a parent are similar to their reactions to a stranger. About 20 percent of children have formed this type of attachment.

An anxious-resistant attachment is likely to develop when parents are inconsistent—sometimes responsive to their child's signals and sometimes not. The child tends to become upset when a parent leaves but ambivalent upon return. When the parent returns, the child may move toward the parent but have difficulty establishing closeness. About 10 percent of children form this type of attachment.

A spectrum of parental behaviors has been shown to be associated with infants who develop a disorganized/disoriented type of attachment. According to the *Encyclopedia on Early Childhood Development*, "These behaviours include parental withdrawal, negative-intrusive responses, role-confused responses, disoriented responses and frightened or frightening behaviours. The spectrum also includes affective communication errors, such as contradictory responses to infant signals and failure to respond to clear affective signals from the infant."[55] The behavior of a child with a disorganized/disoriented attachment is inconsistent. At times, the child may happily approach the parent as a securely attached infant would, and at other times the child may avoid or "freeze" when near the parent.

Psychologist Harry Harlow demonstrated that in addition to responsiveness to the baby's needs, tactile contact is important in the attachment process.[56] Working with young rhesus monkeys, Harlow demonstrated that tactile contact provided by a surrogate mother was even more important than food in forming emotional attachments. Harlow separated young monkeys from their mothers and gave them a choice of being "raised" either by a soft terry-cloth surrogate mother that provided no food or a wire surrogate mother that provided food from an attached baby bottle. The monkeys chose to spend much of their time clinging to the terry-cloth mother and very little time in contact with the wire mother, except for feeding periods. The monkeys got very upset when their terry-cloth mother was removed but not when their wire mother was removed. Only the terry-cloth mother provided comfort, security, and a safe base from which to explore.

Subsequent research has found that motion also plays a role in attachment.[57] In summary, Harlow's research suggests that holding, hugging, cuddling, and rocking infants will help in the formation of a secure attachment.

WHY IS IT IMPORTANT FOR PARENTS TO LEARN ABOUT NORMAL CHILD DEVELOPMENT AND TECHNIQUES OF PARENTING?

Many people believe that parenting should come naturally and that parent education programs are not needed. They often point out that *they* turned out okay and their parents didn't have any formal parent education. As pointed out in chapter one, "Getting Ready to Become a Parent," helping a child develop into a productive adult is a very complicated process, requiring an ever-changing and diverse set of skills. Participating in a parent-education program or educating yourself by reading books or attending parenting workshops or classes can help you understand the challenges and complexities of parenting and better prepare you to handle them, as well as help you to identify any aspects of your child's development that may not be normal.

With the exception of parenting, few people would take on a complicated task without some education or training. Like parenting, building a house is a complicated process that requires a diverse set of skills. Just as it wouldn't be wise to start constructing a house without first educating yourself about the process and acquiring the necessary skills, it isn't a good idea to start to raise a child without doing the same. Educating yourself about parenting and normal child development will increase the chances that your parenting efforts will be successful.

According to an article in *ScienceDaily*, "Almost one-third of U.S. parents have a surprisingly low-level knowledge of typical infant development and unrealistic expectations for their child's physical, social and emotional growth."[58] Parent-education programs, parenting books, and parenting workshops and courses typically focus on helping parents to better understand fundamental elements of parenting, including the basics of normal child development, the importance of early stimulation, approaches to discipline, the use of behavior-modification techniques, and the use of techniques for building self-esteem. They also teach communication and problem-solving skills. They also help parents understand that blaming a child for misbehavior isn't an effective way to change that behavior. People who have been educated on parenting practices come to understand that in order to change a child's behavior, the parent's behavior must first change.

Parenting-education programs are beneficial for all parents, although many of them target high-risk parents, including those who are young, poor, single, and have little education. Programs that are particularly designed for high-risk parents also include information on health, nutrition, and safety. Parents who participate in these training programs become more confident and capable parents, and their children tend to be healthier, be better adjusted emotionally, have better social skills, and score higher on measures of intelligence. [59, 60]

How should parents go about selecting a child-care arrangement?

Because of the large number of single-parent families and families with two working parents, according to 2005 US Census Bureau Data only about 20 percent of children under the age of five were being cared for by a parent; about 25 percent were being cared for by relatives, primarily grandparents, which leaves about 50 percent being cared for by a non-family member.[61] Non-family arrangements include child-care centers, nursery schools, preschools, in-home care, and federally funded Head Start programs.

While cost and convenience are important considerations in selecting a child-care arrangement, the quality of care should be the primary concern. The child's needs and personality, and what each available child-care arrangement offers, should be considered before making a decision. The quality of all arrangements, even those that are licensed, should be investigated. A major study of 400 licensed child-care facilities was conducted over a two-and-a-half-year period by researchers from the University of Colorado at Denver, the University of California at Los Angeles, the University of North Carolina, and Yale University.[62] This "Cost, Quality, and Child Outcomes" study report found that the vast majority of the centers met health and safety standards, but the quality of the child care was "sufficiently poor to interfere with children's emotional and intellectual development." Only 8 percent of infant classrooms and 24 percent of preschool classrooms were judged good or excellent in quality. This is a result of the fact that the licensing process focuses on health and safety standards rather than the quality of care being provided.

There are several reasons why good quality child-care is not the norm. Most people who work in the child-care field are not well-educated. They typically know little about children and child development; they gain most of their knowledge through on-the-job experience. Because most day-care-center workers are poorly paid, day-care centers typically have a high staff turnover rate, which means that staff members typically lack experience and often leave before gaining much knowledge or getting to know the children well.

In selecting a child-care arrangement, it is important to find out about the education/training of the caregiver(s). It is also important to pay a visit while children are being cared for. If visits are discouraged, look for another arrangement. During the visit, in addition to checking to see if the facility is safe and clean, attention should be paid to the schedule of activities and available learning materials, the staff-to-child ratio, and the sensitivity and responsiveness of the caregivers. If food is provided, a menu should be checked to see if it meets basic nutritional standards. Parents should also ask if children are supervised at all times, even when they are sleeping, and about the rules and how rule violations are dealt with. Finally, parents should also talk with the parents of children who currently are being cared for at the facility.

Even if you are a stay-at-home parent caring for your young child, it is important for your child to spend time interacting with other children. This can be accomplished in a number of ways, including arranging playdates, caring for other children in your home, or having your child attend a preschool or day-care center on part-time basis. Spending time with other children, especially in someone else's care, will help your child develop social skills and become independent. Also, high-quality day-care centers and preschools provide a highly stimulating environment, which enhances cognitive development.

About the time my first child was two years old, I began to investigate the child-care options that were available in the area in which I live. Finding none that seemed to me to be able to meet both the intellectual and emotional needs of young children, and being aware of how important the early years are for later development, I along with two other professors founded a Montessori preschool, which is still in operation today. The Montessori approach to education was developed by Maria Montessori, the first female to become a medical doctor in Italy. She believed that children have a natural desire to learn, and learn best when allowed to work at their own pace (explore) in a carefully prepared (stimulating) environment. The new Montessori School teacher I mentioned in the example above who was pressuring my daughter to develop her language skills wasn't following the Montessori philosophy, in which children should primarily be self-directed in their learning.

In a carefully controlled study, the Montessori approach to education has been found to be more effective in several dimensions than the traditional approach. A *Science* article on the study quotes the researchers as saying, "On several dimensions, children at a public inner-city Montessori school had superior outcomes relative to a sample of Montessori applicants who, because of a random lottery, attended other schools. By the end of kindergarten, the Montessori children performed better on standardized tests of reading and math, engaged in positive interaction on the playground more, and showed advanced social cognition and executive control more. They also showed more concern for fairness and justice. At the end of elementary school, Montessori children wrote more creative essays with more complex sentence structures, selected more positive responses to social dilemmas, and reported feeling more of a sense of community at their school."[63]

SUMMARY

To insure that children receive the best possible start, good prenatal and early postnatal care is essential, including good nutrition and the avoidance of exposure to toxic substances like alcohol, lead, pesticides and tobacco smoke. In addition, a highly stimulating environment should be provided in which children are encouraged, but not forced, to explore. It is also important for parents to be both sensitive and responsive to their infants so that a secure attachment is formed. Finally, parents should educate themselves about normal child development and parenting techniques, and carefully explore all child-care options before making a selection.

Chapter 3
Building Self-Esteem

- What is the difference between self-concept and self-esteem?
- Why doesn't a positive self-concept always lead to a high level of self-esteem?
- What are the benefits of having a high level of self-esteem?
- What can parents do to foster the development of their children's self-esteem?
    a. Provide a safe and secure environment
    b. Always be respectful
    c. Use descriptive feedback
    d. Be a positive role model
    e. Express confidence in children
    f. Challenge any incorrect negative self-statements children make
- Why is it important that praise be well-earned?
- Why should parents focus more on children's efforts than accomplishments?
- Why is it important to teach children to be polite to all, but to not automatically respect (or disrespect) anyone?
- Why are children high in self-esteem more likely to become self-directed and caring adults?

WHAT IS THE DIFFERENCE BETWEEN SELF-CONCEPT AND SELF-ESTEEM?

Self-concept refers to the qualities and characteristics that you ascribe to yourself. For example, do you see yourself as male or female, young or old, stupid or smart, or athletic or nonathletic? Your self-concept is initially formed by feedback from others, and later from direct experience. Initially, a parent may tell a child that he/she is very smart, but ultimately that child's concept of just how bright he/she is will often, but not always, be based on his/her direct observations—seeing how he/she compares with relatives, friends, classmates, etc.

Self-esteem refers to how you feel about our self-concept. Do you feel good or bad about being male or female, young or old, dumb or smart, or athletic or nonathletic? Your self-esteem is initially based on the value that others, especially your parents, place on your qualities and characteristics, and later by the value that you place on them. For example, two children from different families are both good athletes. The parents of one family highly value athletic ability and make a big fuss over their child's athletic talent. Hence that child's self-esteem is boosted by athleticism. The parents of the other family don't place much value on athletic skill and say little about their child's athletic talent. Hence that child's self-esteem doesn't benefit nearly as much from athletic skill.

As the two children grow up and go out in the world, they will typically decide for themselves just how important athletic ability is. Perhaps the child who came from the family that stressed the importance of athletic talent will eventually decide that there are many other more important talents worth possessing, and athletic ability will come to play a much smaller role in determining self-esteem. Perhaps the child who came from the family that didn't place much value on athletic talent will eventually decide that athleticism is extremely important, and hence athletic ability will come to play a much larger role in determining self-esteem.

WHY DOESN'T A POSITIVE SELF-CONCEPT ALWAYS LEAD TO A HIGH LEVEL OF SELF-ESTEEM?

How a person feels about him/herself in total is known as his/her overall or global self-esteem. How a person feels about parts of him/

herself is known as domain-specific self-esteem. If a person has a high degree of self-esteem in all of the domains that he/she considers to be important, global self-esteem will be high. If a person has a low degree of self-esteem in even one domain that he/she particularly values, global self-esteem may be low, despite the presence of many wonderful talents and abilities.[1] For example, many people are aware of a well-known, highly successful, and multitalented talk-show host who suffers from low global self-esteem because of a body-weight problem. In the society we live in, many people, especially women, believe that being attractive is of crucial importance. It is very difficult for any woman who highly values appearance and is considerably overweight to feel good about who she is, regardless of how many other positive characteristics she knows that she possesses.

In addition to intelligence, athletic ability, and appearance, there is also a tendency in our society for relationships and wealth to be highly valued. Since relatively few children posses all of the things they value, or don't possess them to the degree that they desire, many suffer from low global self-esteem. Parents may not be aware of this because they may not think that possessing all of these things is nearly as important as their children do, or perhaps parents have lower standards of what are acceptable levels of these things to possess. Two personal stories come to mind, both involving college students I taught many years ago. In both cases, after getting to know me over the course of many months, each acknowledged that she suffered from low global self-esteem. To my surprise, in each case, what appeared to me to be a strength that each possessed turned out to be a self-perceived "weakness" and was the reason for the low overall self-esteem.

The first case involved a young woman who seemed to me to have it all. She was very bright and did very well academically. She had wonderful interpersonal skills and was interesting to talk with. I believe that she was also a varsity athlete. I judged her to come from a family that was at least financially comfortable. Perhaps her most outstanding characteristic was her stunning beauty. Over time I got to know her quite well, and was puzzled because she appeared to me to have a relatively low level of self-esteem. One day I asked her about that and was absolutely shocked by her answer. She told me that because of her appearance, she didn't feel all that good about herself. Since I was absolutely unaware of any flaws whatsoever in her appearance, this totally caught me by surprise. When I asked her to talk a bit about her appearance, she told me that she knew that she was attractive based on most people's standards, but not based upon her own. I then asked her where she thought she stood in appearance with regard to the other thousand or so women on campus; did she think she was in the top half or top quarter? To my continued amazement she said, "I believe that I am number six or seven." Thinking that I might have misheard her, I said, "Do you mean that there are only five or six better looking women on this campus?" She answered yes, and proceeded to name the women who she thought were more attractive. As our discussion continued, she told me that her family highly valued appearance, and that she had other family members who were more attractive than she was. In this case, a very beautiful woman's self-esteem suffered because she didn't meet her own unrealistically high standard of beauty. This was certainly not something that any observer would have anticipated.

The second case involved another young woman who seemed to have a lot going for her but suffered from low self-esteem. She too was a bright and capable student, and she came from a very wealthy family. After completing a parenting course with me, she would often drop by my office just to chat. Based on our conversations, I began to see that she suffered from low self-esteem. She eventually told me that her low self-esteem was primarily based on the fact that she wasn't very bright. Since she did very well in my course and clearly appeared quite bright to me, I was puzzled. I eventually asked her why she believed that she wasn't all that bright. In response, she mentioned that she thought that other family members and some of her friends were brighter than she was. When I asked if she had ever taken an IQ test, she told me that she had done so on three occasions. Since I was fairly sure that she must have scored reasonably high, I asked her what scores she had received. She immediately answered, "Those tests don't matter anyway." With some additional encouragement, she finally told me that on all three tests she had scored around 140. When I told her that those were high scores, placing her in about the top 1 percent of the population, she said that she had learned as much in an introductory psychology course she had taken, but once again said to me that she didn't believe in IQ tests. Over the next couple of months, it became clear to me that her feeling that she was not all that bright stemmed from having received lots of critical feedback from her parents throughout her entire life.

Both of these cases illustrate that a person's self-esteem doesn't always closely relate to their actual abilities and characteristics, and to the way others see them. Both cases also illustrate that many people have unrealistically high standards, often stemming from what they were told about their abilities or characteristics when they were young. Unfortunately, many children grow up hearing that they are not quite "good" enough. They may hear their parents say "do your best," but they somehow know what they really mean is "be the best (prettiest, smartest, and so on)." Sometimes this stems from hearing over and over again "if you only tried harder you would do better (be thinner, get higher grades, and so on)," even though they may already be trying very hard. It may also stem from hearing "What's wrong with you, why can't you do well like your sister (or your cousin)?" Hearing these kinds of statements may leave children with feelings of inadequacy, even when they are quite capable. If a child is really trying hard, it is very important for parents to accept whatever level of accomplishment they are able to achieve. In the highly competitive society we live in, most parents find doing that to be very difficult, if not impossible.

WHAT ARE THE BENEFITS OF HAVING A HIGH LEVEL OF SELF-ESTEEM?

Self-esteem influences emotions, motivations, attitudes, thoughts, and behaviors. Children with high global self-esteem think well of themselves and are generally happy, optimistic, confident, and independent. They also tend to be comfortable taking on new challenges and have a relatively easy time handling conflict and coping with all kinds of pressure, including pressure from peers. In addition, social adjustment, academic achievement, and vocational goals are linked to global self-esteem.[2]

Children with low global self-esteem think poorly of themselves and are generally unhappy, pessimistic, lacking in confidence, and dependent.[3] They also tend to be fearful of new challenges, experience considerable anxiety when dealing with conflict, and often succumb to pressure from others. Low self-esteem is also associated with depression and negative self-statements, such as "I'm no good," "I'll never be able to do it," or I'm a loser." Finally, compared to adolescents with high self-esteem, those with low self-esteem have been found to have poorer mental and physical health, and as adults are more likely to engage in criminal behavior.[4]

Global self-esteem is associated with risk-taking behavior in adolescents.[5] Male and female adolescents who are low in global self-esteem have an increased likelihood of suicide ideation and behaviors. Female adolescents with low global self-esteem are more likely to engage in risky sexual behavior, and male adolescents who are low in global self-esteem are more like to be bullied and to use alcohol. The components of global self-esteem that have been found to be the best predictors of adolescent risk-taking behavior are low self-esteem with respect to family and school.[6] Not surprisingly, low peer self-esteem is the component of self-esteem most closely associated with adolescents being bullied. However, adolescents who score low in peer self-esteem are less likely to engage in some types of risk-taking behaviors, possibly because they spend less time with peers and hence have fewer opportunities to be "tempted."

WHAT CAN PARENTS CAN DO TO FOSTER THE DEVELOPMENT OF THEIR CHILDREN'S SELF-ESTEEM?

Provide a safe and secure environment

In 1943, Abraham Maslow, one of the founders of humanistic psychology, proposed a theory of human motivation that was based on a needs hierarchy.[7] His theory is still widely accepted today. Maslow believed that a person had to have their lower needs at least minimally satisfied before they could move on to meeting higher needs. Before esteem needs (feeling accepted and respected by others and by oneself) could be met, a person had to sequentially first have their physiological needs (hunger, thirst, sleep), safety needs (feeling safe and secure in a predictable world), and social needs (belonging to a family and feeling loved) met. For example, a child with an unmet physiological need, such as hunger, will devote all of his/her energy to getting this need met, even if it means risking the need for safety by stealing to obtain food. As discussed in chapter two, "Giving Children the Best Possible Start," when parents are highly responsive to meeting young children's needs, a secure attachment between the child and parent is formed. This secure attachment is the foundation for meeting the child's physiological, safety, and social needs, and allows him/her to move toward meeting esteem needs. At the top of Maslow's needs hierarchy is the need to become self-actualized, which will be discussed toward the end of this chapter.

Always be respectful

There are times when angry parents say hurtful things to their children that they know are disrespectful, such as "I wish you were never born" or "How did I end up with a rotten kid like you?" Clearly, statements like this bring down a child's self-esteem. Anger without insult should be a goal for every parent. Should this goal ever be violated, a sincere apology should follow. Later in this chapter, in the section dealing with "Be a positive role model," apologizing will be dealt with in detail.

There are other times when parents are disrespectful to their children without even realizing it. The tone of their voice and the statements they make often discount or belittle their children's feelings and thoughts. We often hear parents say things like, "Don't make such a big fuss, that can't hurt very much," "When are you going to grow up?" or "It's stupid to be afraid of the dark." Because we hear statements like this so often, we don't pay much attention to them, and as a result we often fail to realize that they are disrespectful. How would you feel if you fell down and were hurting and a friend said to you, "Don't make such a big fuss, that can't hurt very much," or if you were upset over something and a friend said to you, "When are you going to grow up?" or if you had a fear of something and a friend said, "It's stupid to be afraid." Clearly, these statements would be upsetting to you because they are disrespectful and belittling. Children often experience these statements in the same way. Children's self-esteem suffers when they don't feel respected.

Hearing such statements can cause children to question their own feelings and thoughts. They may wonder, should they be feeling afraid in the dark, or should they be upset when they fall down? If a child loses confidence in their thoughts and feelings, their protective defenses become weakened. Someday they may find themselves in a situation where they are feeling uncomfortable and thinking something isn't right. Such a situation might involve an adult who is asking them to do something that they are not sure they should do. If the children's feelings and thoughts have been respected in the past, they will likely trust them now, not obey the adult, and remove themselves from the situation. If the children have come to question what they feel and think, they will be more likely to do what the adult is requesting and less capable of providing self-protection.

Another way that parents convey disrespect for a child is when they prohibit the child from spending time in some portion of the house, or prohibit the child from sitting in a special chair. How would you feel as an adult if your friend didn't allow you to enter their living room or asked you to get out of a chair that they preferred to sit in? Many years ago, my in-laws gave my family a beautiful antique dining-room table and a set of antique wooden chairs. Having somewhat of a temperamental back, I found that the chairs were not very comfortable for me. Eventually I decided that I needed to get a different chair, because I was tired of having a sore back. So I purchased a very comfortable but unattractive and inexpensive metal-framed chair. My wife wasn't very happy with my decision, because the new chair stood out like a sore thumb next to the antique chairs. One day my younger daughter, who at the time was about seven, sat in the chair and said, "Boy, Dad, this chair is a lot more comfortable than those wooden chairs. I wish I had a chair like this." I could have easily just ignored her statement or said, "You're just a kid, the wooden chairs are good enough for you because you don't have a problem with your back," but doing either would have been disrespectful. So, to respect my daughter's wishes, I felt I had two choices: either share my chair with her or purchase another for her to use. I ended up purchasing an identical chair for her, and unfortunately made my wife even more unhappy.

Often parents are very busy and, as a result, they don't give their children their full attention during conversations. At the time a child wants to talk, the parent may be busy with some household task, or perhaps working on their computer, or maybe just relaxing, watching TV, or reading a book. Just as it would be disrespectful to continue to engage in these activities if a friend wanted to talk with you, it is disrespectful to continue to engage in these activities if a child wants to talk with you. Stopping what you are doing and making eye contact with the child communicates that you believe what they have to say is important. Another option that also shows respect would be to say, "I'm really busy right now, but in ten minutes let's talk."

Children often follow the lead of their parents. Parents who care about and show respect for their children's thoughts and feelings are likely to raise children who are empathetic and considerate of others. Parents who disrespect their child's thoughts and feelings are likely to raise children who are more self-centered and inconsiderate. Respect is a two-way street.

Use descriptive feedback

Feedback from parents and other family members is the most important factor shaping the self-esteem of young children. The amount and nature of praise and criticism that a child receives will initially determine feelings of self-worth. Unfortunately, many parents and caretakers tend to pay more attention to misbehavior than to desirable behavior. They are much more likely to catch a child being bad than being good. If a child is playing quietly, often nothing is said. But if a child is making a ruckus, almost always something critical will be communicated. It is difficult for a child who frequently hears criticism and seldom hears praise to develop a positive sense of self. Therefore, it is important to focus on catching children being good. By acknowledging good behavior, parents not only have an impact on their child's self-esteem, but they also increase the probability that the good behavior will occur more frequently.

Most parents tend to use evaluative praise. They say things like, "You played well in the game today" or "That's a wonderful picture you painted." While evaluative statements of praise help to build self-esteem, they don't work nearly as well as descriptive statements of praise. Describing to a child why they played well or what you liked about the picture they painted is more informative, and lets the child know that you paid close attention to what they did. Saying "You really kept your eye on the ball today" or "The colors you chose makes your picture really come alive" provides the child with useful information. Evaluative praise also tends to be limiting.[8] If a child hears that he/she is already a great player or a wonderful artist, there is little reason for the child to try to improve. He/she is more likely to be motivated to work at becoming a better player or artist if descriptive praise is used.

Using descriptive praise also takes some of the pressure to perform off of the child. If children frequently hear that they are great or wonderful, they may feel pressure to continue to always be great or wonderful. During times when they are not, they may be concerned that they are disappointing their parents.

Children who only hear lots of praise from their parents may come to wonder if that praise is sincere and accurate. They may come to the conclusion that their parents are not being objective. Children who receive a little bit of criticism mixed in with lots of praise are less likely to question the sincerity and accuracy of the praise. Descriptive criticism is not only more effective than evaluative criticism, but it is also less likely to weaken self-esteem. Providing evaluative criticism by telling children that they played terribly or that their painting is awful provides little useful information, and is likely to weaken their self-esteem. By comparison, providing descriptive criticism by saying to a child "I think you didn't keep your eye on the ball today" or "Your choice of colors makes it difficult to see the various elements in the picture" provides useful information and is much less likely to lower self-esteem.

Providing descriptive praise and descriptive criticism also helps the child to better understand how to judge performance. This is important, because it is advantageous for children to be able to evaluate their own performance and not be dependent on others to decide if they did well or poorly. As will be discussed at the end of this chapter, children need to be able to judge their own performance if they are to become self-directed and self-actualized.

Be a positive role model

A young child generally looks up to his/her parents and learns many things by observing both their behavior and the things they say, including how they evaluate themselves. If parents are always putting themselves down, harshly criticizing their own weaknesses and rarely pointing out their strengths, their children are also likely to dwell on personal weakness as well. Focusing on weaknesses and not acknowledging strengths leads to low self-esteem. On the other hand, it isn't good for parents to only focus on their strengths and not acknowledge their weaknesses. If parents do this, it is likely that their child will come to see them as close to being perfect, and in turn believe that it is important for him/her to be perfect as well. Every time that the child realizes that isn't so, self-esteem will suffer. If parents are able to acknowledge their strengths and not try to hide their weakness, and at the same time communicate that they feel good about themselves, their children will likely learn to do the same.

Another way to help a child to understand that it is okay not to be perfect is for a parent to apologize to a child for doing something that negatively affected the child for which the parent is sorry. Some parents are reluctant to apologize for fear that if they do they will lose the respect of the child, since apology acknowledges a failing or a mistake. However, as long as the apology is sincere and the parent is not frequently doing things for which an apology is necessary, the parent will actually gain the respect of the child. If parents take the time to think about and then explain why they are sorry for what they did and how they wished they would have handled the situation, apologizing can be a learning experience for both the parent and the child. It will also make it much easier for the child to acknowledge his/her own failings or mistakes—and, when appropriate, apologize for them.

While apologizing is encouraged, asking a child for forgiveness isn't. When a parent asks a child for forgiveness, the parent is putting him/herself at the mercy of the child. This is basically a role reversal, where the child is being put in charge of the outcome instead of the parent. If the child chooses not to forgive the parent, perhaps because he/she is still angry or because the parent has repeated the same mistake many times, the child will likely feel guilty and the parent will likely be upset with the child. Also, just to please the parent, children may feel "forced" to offer forgiveness even though they really don't want to. Forcing children to say something that they don't believe is essentially encouraging them to lie, and should be discouraged.

Parents should also role-model and discuss why it isn't important to be the best, as long as you do your best. This helps children feel good even if they are not top performers. When my daughters were young children, they liked to watch me run around the track. Although I worked very hard at running, I was only an average runner. However, because I was able to run much faster and farther than they could, they were convinced that I was an outstanding runner. One day I decided that I was going to enter a local ten-kilometer race. My daughters were very excited and told me that they expected me to win. I tried to explain to them that although I enjoyed running and ran a lot, I was only an average runner, and there was no chance that I was going to win the race. Based on comments they made on the day of the race, it appeared that they still expected me to win. Although I was very happy with my race-day performance, they were just about in tears when I finished about twelfth out of about forty runners. However, because they saw how pleased I was about running a good personal time, my daughters learned that being the best was not nearly as important as doing your best, and that enjoyment can come even from doing something that you aren't particularly good at.

About ten years later, my older daughter went out for her high-school soccer team. Although she was a good runner, she wasn't particularly skilled at soccer and didn't get much playing time in games. However, our family supported her and attended every game. I was pleased to see that she enjoyed being part of the team, despite receiving little playing time. I believe that part of the reason she was able to do so was because early in life she had learned an important lesson by observing how I dealt with my race performance. She later switched from the soccer team to the track-and-field team, where did considerably better; in her senior year, she won a 1500-meter race in a dual-county track meet. She was certainly happy with her track performance, but because being the best was never something that was stressed, she certainly wasn't overjoyed.

Finally, parents need to model and discuss a wide range of values and characteristics, such as honesty and integrity, flexibility and compromise, kindness and empathy, politeness and courtesy, commitment and perseverance, and independence and autonomy. People who posses these values and characteristics have much to be proud of and are likely to be looked up to by others, and hence are likely to have a high level of self-esteem.

Express confidence in children

When a parent says to a child things like, "You're too young to understand," "You're not big enough to do that," or "You will make too big a mess if you help me cook," the parent coveys a lack of confidence in the child's abilities. This isn't good for the child's self-esteem. On the other hand, when a parent says to a child, "This is complicated, but since you have a good head on your shoulders, I bet you will be able to understand," or "This is difficult to do, so let's work on it together," or "Sure you can help me with some parts of the cooking," the parent conveys confidence in the child, and this helps build the child's self esteem.

Allowing children to make their own decisions is another way of conveying confidence. Even young children can make decisions, such as picking out what they are going to wear. If the child is very young, the parent can let the child choose from several outfits that the parent feels are appropriate for the occasion and weather conditions. A parent can also have a child help decide what will be served for dinner. The parent might say, "We are going to have chicken tonight, but you can choose which vegetable we are going to have with the chicken. We have peas, broccoli, and string beans in the refrigerator. Which would you like to have tonight?" There are many other types of decisions that parents often make but that children are certainly capable of making or at least helping to make, such as choosing the color that their room will be painted, deciding when to do their homework, or deciding what kinds of after-school activities they want to participate in.

How you handle giving money to a child can convey confidence or a lack of confidence in the child's ability to make decisions. Children who do not receive an allowance need to ask their parents for money when they want to buy something for themselves or for someone else. This puts the parents in the position of deciding if the child can make the purchase. Children who receive an allowance are able to decide for themselves if they want to use their allowance money to make a purchase. When a child buys a present for a friend or family member with money saved from an allowance, they will feel much prouder than when making a purchase using money that a parent gives at the time of the purchase. If you want to raise a self-directed child, you need to give the child opportunities to make decisions. Giving a child an allowance is one way to accomplish that. Chapter six, "Parenting Adolescents," includes a thorough discussion of the advantages and disadvantages of giving an allowance.

Overprotective parents who all too quickly come to the aid or defense of their children are communicating a lack of confidence in their children's ability to solve a problem or to provide self-protection. In some situations, the measure of a good parent is what he/she is *not* willing to do for his/her child.[9] By not rushing to the aid of a child, you are signaling to the child that you have confidence in his/her ability to handle things. For example, many parents find it difficult to see their child struggling over a difficult and time-consuming school project, and as a result either do part of the project for the child or complain to the child's teacher. Instead, they should acknowledge the child's frustration about the project and then encourage the child to work out a plan to complete the project in the time allotted. If the child and parent both feel that an insufficient amount of time has been allotted for the project, then the parent should encourage the child to speak with the teacher about negotiating an extension for the class.

Many devoted parents go out of their way to make life easier for their children by doing things for them. We have all heard parents say, "Let me do that for you honey" or "Let me help you with that." When these words are said regarding a task that the child knows he/she is fully capable of accomplishing alone, they communicate a lack of confidence in the child and in a way encourage the child to become dependent on the parent rather than independent and self-directed. This is another example where the measure of a good parent is what he/she is not willing to do for his/her child. When children are encouraged to do things for themselves, they learn to become functionally independent. In the parenting seminars I teach, on many occasions college students have said that when they first arrived on campus they felt terribly lost because they had never learned how to do things for themselves, such as make a bed, do laundry, or handle a checking account. While this probably isn't too surprising, there are some students who have been brave enough to share the fact that they were not even capable of doing some of the most basic things. The most shocking example was a student who told the class that to this very day, her parents always cut up her meat, even when they eat out in restaurants! Needless to say, this was a student who didn't have high self-esteem because her parents often communicated a lack of confidence in her abilities.

Emotional independence, which is quite separate from functional independence, also needs to be fostered. Some students arrive on campus knowing how to do very little but are quite comfortable being away from home. Others arrive on campus knowing how to do almost everything but find it extremely difficult to be on their own. They need the emotional support of their parents and/or friends in order to be able to function well. In my experience, far too few students begin college both functionally and emotionally independent. Just like functional independence, emotional independence should be fostered early in life. Overprotective parents often struggle with this. I observed a prime example many years ago when I was dropping off my younger daughter at the Montessori preschool I helped to found, which is located on the Alfred University campus where I teach.

Another father was dropping off his three-year-old son for the boy's first day at the preschool. As soon as the boy took off his coat, he immediately went over to see what some other children were doing who had arrived a bit earlier. The father clearly appeared to me to be much more anxious than his son. Worried that the child would be upset after he left, he approached his son and asked him to come over to the cubby where the boy's coat and other things had been placed. The boy clearly wanted to stay and watch the other children, but reluctantly went with his father. The father said, "After I leave, you may feel sad and upset. If you do, here is where your blanket will be kept, and you can come get it and use it to comfort yourself." Over ten years later, I was at a picnic and noticed something about to fall out of the back pocket of this boy, who now really was a young man. When I pointed out that he was about to lose something, he quickly shoved the item back in his pocket and his face turned red from embarrassment. His father later told me that it was a piece of his baby blanket that he still carried with him. While I can't be sure, I believe that this is a case of a child who had difficulty with emotional independence because his parents were overprotective, and from a very early age communicated that they didn't have confidence in his ability to take care of himself. This kind of a message certainly doesn't help a child's self-esteem.

Helping children to become functionally independent primarily involves having them learn how to do many different things and giving them many opportunities to practice doing them. This of course requires parents to stand back and resist the urge to do things for their children. Helping children to become emotionally independent has some parallels but is a bit more complicated. To accomplish this, it is helpful for parents to communicate in a variety of ways that they have confidence in their children, including their ability to learn how to feel comfortable without their parents' presence. This should begin early in life, by having children learn to sleep in their own bed in their own room, and by having them learn how to feel comfortable in the care of others. Many parents struggle with these things because they have trouble seeing their child upset or unhappy, which typically happens early on. As children get older, they should be encouraged to spend longer and longer periods of time away from their parents by joining groups or clubs, sleeping over at friends' and relatives' houses, and eventually staying with friends or relatives for more extended visits. If resources allow, an excellent way to help children become comfortable on their own is for them to attend a summer sleep-away camp. However, unless steps have been taken to help establish a basic level of emotional independence, sending a child to a sleep-away camp can be traumatizing.

Challenge any incorrect negative self-statements children make

Negative self-statements, especially exaggerated ones, weaken self-esteem and are associated with depression. Children are often prone to making such statements. When they do so, a parent should challenge their thinking. For example, a child who is having trouble with one subject at school is likely to say, either out loud or to him/herself, "I'm stupid" or "I'm a failure at school." If parents become aware of this exaggerated negative talk or self-talk, they should first express to the child that they understand that he/she is upset and then point out that what the child is saying is inaccurate. They should then encourage the child to make a more accurate statement, such as "I'm doing well in all but one school subject."

Often, exaggerated negative self-statements occur in connection with a child disliking something about his/her appearance. Instead of saying, "I wish I had a better complexion," the child might say, "My face is ugly"; or instead of saying, "I wish I didn't have heavy thighs," the child might say, "I'm a fat pig." In addition to challenging inaccurate statements children make about their appearance, parents need to be careful that they are not behaving in ways that increase the child's focus on appearance. Parents who make statements in front of their children like "Does my butt look big in this outfit?" "Do I look good in this color?" or "Do stripes make me look fat?" are communicating that appearance is very important. This increases the chances that their children will be critical of their own appearance. Spending a great deal of time and money shopping for clothes, going to tanning salons, or having cosmetic surgery are some of the many other ways that parents model the importance of appearance. It is best if parents are careful not to contribute to the tremendous emphasis that society already places on appearance. The example given earlier in this chapter of the young woman who was very beautiful but suffered from low-self esteem because she felt she wasn't the *most* beautiful is an example of the overemphasis often placed on appearance.

Many years ago, a student I knew who had low self-esteem told me that she was terribly unhappy with her appearance because she was "grossly overweight." Since she clearly had a distorted body-image, I asked her why she felt that way. She answered, "Because I look awful in anything I wear." I told her that I was surprised that she felt that way, and that I didn't see her that way. However, recognizing that body-image distortion is an extremely difficult thing to change, I decided to use a technique that I had read about to try to help her gain a more realistic picture of her appearance. Starting with her feet and moving slowly up her body to her head, I asked her to describe each body part in terms of amount of excess fat. To make a long story short, all but one part of her body she either described as lean or muscular, and that part was her breasts, which she said were far too large. Because she was telling herself that she was "grossly overweight" instead of saying "My body is lean and muscular, but my breasts are large," her self-esteem suffered. Over time, I believe that I helped her to change her self-talk, and as a result, she began to feel a little better about herself—although a number of years later she wrote to me that she'd had breast reduction surgery and was now very happy with her appearance.

Many of the above suggestions for building children's self-esteem are consistent with an authoritative type of parenting style, which is described in detail in chapter four, "Discipline and Parenting Styles." Adolescents who have been raised using an authoritative parenting style have been found to have considerably higher levels of self-esteem than adolescents raised using other types of parenting styles.

WHY IS IT IMPORTANT THAT PRAISE BE WELL-EARNED?

While having a high level of self-esteem is associated with many positive outcomes, parents should be cautioned against providing their child with an overinflated level of self-esteem. Self-esteem is the perception of oneself. When that perception doesn't come close to matching reality, problems are likely to develop. When children receive frequent praise for mediocre performance, they may begin to think about themselves in ways that don't match reality. When they are out in the real world, they may be shocked when they find out that they are not nearly as terrific as they had been led to believe. Examples of this include parents who tell children with average talent that they are terrific artists or skilled musicians. Another example of conveying a false sense of accomplishment occurs in some youth sports leagues, where every player on every team receives a tournament trophy regardless of how the team placed in the competition. Since children need to learn to acknowledge and accept both their successes and their failures, it would be better to only have members of the top team(s) receive trophies, and have members of the other teams that didn't do as well receive some more modest memento.

WHY SHOULD PARENTS FOCUS MORE ON CHILDREN'S EFFORTS THAN ACCOMPLISHMENTS?

When a child brings home a report card, performs in a play, or participates in an athletic contest, many parents focus more on the level of accomplishment than on the amount of effort involved. Whether the child does well or poorly, it makes sense to pay more attention to effort than to accomplishment. If you give it some thought, you will realize that there are three primary factors that determine whether someone does well or poorly at anything: genetics, mentoring/instruction/parenting, and effort. If a child excels with little effort, it is largely because of luck; they inherited the right genes and/or were taught by good mentors/instructors/parents. It doesn't make sense to praise children who excel just because they were lucky, but it does make sense to praise children who excel at least in part because of hard work. The reverse is also true—it doesn't make sense to criticize a child who has worked hard but performs poorly. Should we be upset with a child because he/she didn't inherit the right genes or received poor mentoring/instruction/

parenting?

Unfortunately, many parents, teachers, and coaches only convey approval when a child excels. Carl Rogers, a well-known psychotherapist and theorist who was one of the founders of the humanistic approach to psychology, called this *conditional positive regard*.[11] Children learn that they will be loved or appreciated only on the condition that they do well. Unfortunately, this leads children to base their self-worth on their achievements rather than on their efforts. Rogers believed that for children to be happy and reach their full potential (to eventually become self-actualized adults), they need to be given unconditional positive regard. That is, love and appreciation should be given regardless of accomplishments.

WHY IS IT IMPORTANT TO TEACH CHILDREN TO BE POLITE TO ALL, BUT TO NOT AUTOMATICALLY RESPECT (OR DISRESPECT) ANYONE?

Today we often hear people say that because parents are too lenient, children grow up showing a lack of respect for others, especially for adults. Actually, this isn't a bad thing, since respect is something that really should be earned and never automatically granted.

When children are taught to automatically respect someone because of their age, position, wealth, fame, and so on, they are learning that superficial things are what count. This of course has resulted in children blindly respecting and obeying authority figures, some of whom have seriously mistreated them. They are also learning that because they are "just kids," they have to look up to others and they are not yet deserving of respect because they have not achieved age, position, wealth, or fame. This weakens their self-esteem. Instead, we should be teaching children to judge others by their behavior/character. That means that they should be encouraged to evaluate the behavior of their teachers, ministers, coaches, and other adults before deciding if those people are deserving of respect. At the same time, children should be taught to be polite to everyone, regardless of whether that individual has earned their respect. Because good behavior/character is something that all people can have, including children, this then provides children with the opportunity to feel good about who they are as long as they are proud of their behavior/character—thus building their self-esteem.

It is also very important for parents to teach children not to automatically disrespect anyone because of superficial characteristics like age, appearance, position, class, gender, race, religion, nationality, and sexuality. Once again, children should be taught to judge others by their behavior/character. If all parents were to do this, discrimination would dramatically decrease.

One of the ways I have tried to convey this message to both my children and my students is to talk about the people whom I most respect at Alfred University, where I have worked for the past forty-one years. At any university, there are many people with a variety of titles in leadership positions who, by virtue of their positions, are generally respected. However, my children and students all know that I try my best to judge people by their behavior/character and not by superficial characteristics like their position or title. The person who earned my greatest respect, whom I still often talk about in my parenting classes and used to talk about at home when my children were young, is a now-retired janitor. She earned my respect because of how she did her work and how she treated people. Hilda took much more pride in her work than virtually all of the faculty and administrators I know or have known. Our building was always kept in top shape no matter what challenges winter weather in a snowy climate brought. She truly cared about the faculty and the students and knew many of them personally. Although I believe she didn't have a great deal of formal education, she kept current on what was happening in the world and was always willing to briefly stop her work to engage in a discussion. She truly enjoyed her work, and over the many years in which we crossed paths I never once heard her complain about a very heavy workload for which she was receiving relatively little compensation.

WHY ARE CHILDREN HIGH IN SELF-ESTEEM MORE LIKELY TO BECOME SELF-DIRECTED AND CARING ADULTS?

As previously mentioned, a young child's self-esteem is initially based on the amount and type of praise and criticism received from parents and other family members. As the child gets older, feedback from peers becomes a major factor influencing feelings of self-worth. Being well liked by peers and hearing them say positive things boosts self-esteem. Being disliked and picked on by peers lowers self-esteem. Children who have low self-esteem constantly strive to receive positive feedback in order to boost their feelings of self-worth. One obvious way to get that positive feedback is to please others. Often these are the children who succumb to peer pressure, even when they know better. They do so because of their strong need to belong and to be liked.

As children move closer to becoming adults, those with the highest levels of self-esteem are able to begin to base their self-worth more on how *they* feel about who they are than on how their parents or peers feel about who they are. These are the children who are in the process of becoming fully self-directed. According to Maslow, when people are able to meet their physiological, safety, social, and esteem needs (which includes freeing themselves from trying to please others), they are in a position to become self-actualized or to realize their full potential.[12] Self-actualized people are able to acknowledge and accept their own strengths and weaknesses. They also have good character and high moral standards, and are interested in the welfare of others rather than being self-centered.

SUMMARY

Since happiness and success are both tied to self-esteem, it is extremely important for parents to help their children to develop a high level of self-worth. Doing so will also greatly increase the chances that their children will become self-directed and caring people. Providing children with positive feedback, treating them with respect all of the time, and expressing confidence in their abilities are three of the most important things that parents can do to foster the development of self-esteem. If parents mix a little descriptive criticism in with a generous amount of descriptive praise, children are more likely to believe that the praise they are receiving is real and well earned. Parents also need to provide a safe and secure environment, be good role models, and challenge any incorrect negative self-statements their children make. Finally, it is important to teach children to be polite to everyone, but to not automatically respect anyone. They need to learn to judge people by behavior/character and not by superficial characteristics like age, gender, or title.

CHAPTER 4
DISCIPLINE AND PARENTING STYLES

- What should be the primary goal of discipline?
- How do different parenting styles influence children?
  a. Authoritative
  b. Authoritarian
  c. Indulgent
  d. Neglectful
- Why is good communication and role modeling more important than punishment in disciplining children?
- How can the use of rewards dramatically reduce the need for administering punishments?
- What role should punishment play in discipline?
- Why should spanking never be used as a form of discipline?
- What role can natural and logical consequences play in helping to discipline children?
- Why is being consistent important when disciplining children?
- How can reminders help with discipline?
- Why is it important for parents to understand a variety of different parenting techniques and be willing to employ them?

WHAT SHOULD BE THE PRIMARY GOAL OF DISCIPLINE?

The most common form of discipline is punishment, and the most common form of punishment is spanking, which over 90 percent of American parents employ at some time. While young children are more likely to be spanked than older children, just over half of American parents continue to spank children who are twelve years old.[1]

Spanking and other forms of punishment inflict pain and/or unhappiness, and parents who use punishment to discipline do so in the belief that their children will not repeat bad behavior because they will want to avoid being punished. Parents who punish believe this form of discipline to be very effective, frequently citing that when they threaten to punish, whatever misbehavior their children are engaging in immediately stops. What parents who spank or use other forms of punishment fail to consider is what will motivate their children to not to engage in misbehavior when the chances of being caught are slim, and therefore there is little fear of being punished. While punishment and the threat of punishment will stop misbehavior for the moment, neither is effective in producing long-term results, since both focus on instilling fear rather than on teaching values.

The following is an example to illustrate why using fear of punishment fails to teach children what they really should be learning: to be responsible and caring people. Neil Malamuth and his colleagues studied the likelihood of date rape.[2] Across a number of studies, approximately 35 percent of college men reported some likelihood of raping if they could be assured of not being caught and therefore not being punished. Clearly, these men didn't learn what we would hope they would have learned, that using force to take advantage of another person is always wrong, whether or not it will result in punishment. This example should make it clear that controlling misbehavior by fear of punishment is much less desirable than controlling misbehavior by teaching a set of values. We need to discipline in a way that helps children to develop a set of values to guide their behavior, instead of fear of punishment serving as their guide. If we are able to accomplish this, children will be self-disciplined and caring individuals; they will be well-behaved whether or not someone is observing them and can report any misbehavior or administer punishment. This is what every parent should strive to accomplish. Teaching a set of values should be the goal of discipline and is the key to raising a self-directed and caring child.

How do different parenting styles influence children?

One of the most widely accepted ways to classify parenting styles was initially developed by Diana Baumrind.[3, 4, 5] Based on her research, Baumrind described three parenting styles that vary on several important dimensions including responsiveness, nurturance, expectations, control, communication style, and discipline style. Baumrind labeled these styles authoritative, authoritarian, and permissive. Maccoby & Martin expanded the styles to four: authoritative, authoritarian, indulgent (permissive), and neglectful.[6]

Authoritative

Authoritative parents establish rules and guidelines for their children to follow. Because they believe it is important for their children to understand why the rules and guidelines are in place, they take the time to carefully explain them. They are warm and affectionate toward their children and willing to respond to any questions the children may have, allowing the youngsters to challenge the logic behind their policies. They are also flexible and will alter a rule or guideline if a convincing argument is made. They do this because they would much rather use reason and persuasion than power and threats in order to gain compliance, and they want their children to learn how to think for themselves and be responsible for themselves. They would like their children to comply because it is the right thing to do, not out of fear of punishment. As M. L. Jaffe wrote in *Understanding Parenting*, "They want their children to be assertive as well as socially responsible, and self-regulated as well as cooperative."[7] Their approach to discipline can be described as fair and firm. Should reason and persuasion not prevail, they will reluctantly use their parental power in order to gain compliance.

Because authoritative parents convey that they really care about their children and what those children have to say, their parenting style can be described as democratic, with the goal of raising a self-directed child. They are understanding parents, and while encouraging maturity, they are tolerant of their children's age-appropriate behavior. Having always been treated in a kind and respectfully manner, the children of authoritative parents are likely have a high level of self-esteem and grow up to be caring people. Because they have been encouraged to think for themselves, they are also likely to pursue their own interests rather than the interests of their parents or others, such as teachers or coaches. As a result, they tend to be independent and achievement-oriented.[8, 9] However, while a positive relationship between authoritative parenting and high-school achievement is consistently found for children of white families, it is not consistently found for families from all ethnic and cultural backgrounds.[10]

Authoritarian

As described in Amy Chua's recent bestselling book, *The Battle Hymn of the Tiger Mother*, authoritarian parents always want to be in control, and they give a lot of orders and offer few choices. They establish many rules and guidelines for their children to follow, which they strictly enforce. Because they prefer to use power and threats rather than reason and persuasion to gain compliance, they typically don't bother to take the time to carefully explain their policies. When asked a question about a rule or guideline, they typically are not very responsive and are likely to say "Because I said so" or "You should do what I say because I'm your parent." They are strict and inflexible, and don't encourage their children to think for themselves or allow their children to challenge their policies. They believe in keeping children in their place: "seen but not heard." They see parents as superior and children as inferior. They expect their children to comply in order to avoid harsh punishment, and they don't particularly care whether their children believe complying is the right thing to do.

Because they value obedience above all and convey that they are not interested in what their children have to say, this style of parenting can be described as dictatorial. They want their children to be parent-controlled rather than self-controlled. They are not very warm or understanding, and they often expect behavior that would be more appropriate of an older child. All of these things make it likely that their children will also suffer from low self-esteem and be angry and resentful.

Indulgent

Indulgent parents establish few rules and guidelines, and rarely enforce them. They accept and indulge their children's impulses and desires. If their children protest, they typically give in. They often want to avoid confrontation and function more like a friend than a parent. The parents present themselves to their child, according to *Child Development*, "as a resource for him to use as he wishes, not as an ideal for him to emulate, nor as an active agent responsible for shaping or altering his ongoing or future behavior."[11]

Indulgent parents are moderately warm and nurturing, but they're also lenient and provide little supervision, support, or direction to guide their children. Because they have a hands-off approach to parenting and often let their children come and go as they please, without even knowing their whereabouts, their style of parenting can be described as laissez-faire. It isn't unusual for them to expect behavior that would be more appropriate of a younger child. Because of low parental expectations and few parental demands, these children have not been encouraged to reach their full potential and tend to have lower achievement aspirations, lower levels of self-esteem, and issues with self-control.

Neglectful

Neglectful parents tend to be nonresponsive and emotionally detached from their children. They have limited communication with their children and place few demands; they are basically uninvolved and show little interest in their children's development. Except in extreme cases, they do meet their children's basic physiological needs, but provide little emotional support. Children of neglectful parents feel unimportant and rejected, and as would be expected, show the poorest outcomes in all domains.

As the following example shows, parents who employ different parenting styles handle situations very differently. For my tenth birthday, my mother made me a maple-icing birthday cake that tasted absolutely fabulous. The next morning, I wanted a piece for breakfast, but because we had a rule in my house that cake could not be eaten for breakfast (this was long before donuts became a popular breakfast food), I was either going to have to wait until after lunch, when cake could be eaten for dessert, or convince my parents to make a special exception to the rule. Since my parents employed an authoritative parenting style, they were happy to talk with me about any rules that they had in place, and they were also willing to allow rules to be challenged, although they were unlikely to change them unless a very convincing argument could be made. I thought long and hard, because I was determined to not have to wait till after lunch to have some more birthday cake. Eventually, I figured out that the ingredients in a maple-iced cake were quite similar to the ingredients in pancakes served with maple syrup, a breakfast we had about every two or three weeks. Once I pointed out to my parents that the ingredients in pancakes were almost identical to the ingredients in the birthday cake, they agreed to change the "no cake for breakfast" rule. As a result of being able to convince them to change the rule, my self-esteem increased, and I had the best breakfast ever that day.

Had my parents used an authoritarian approach, they would not have allowed any discussion of the rule, and therefore I would not have even attempted to get the rule changed. Had my parents used a permissive parenting style, likely no rules regarding when things could be eaten would have been in place, or if there were some rules, and if I had protested, they would have quickly given in, even if I didn't have a convincing argument for changing the rule. Had my parents been neglectful, they probably wouldn't have gone out of their way to bother to bake a birthday cake, and so the problem wouldn't have existed.

WHY IS GOOD COMMUNICATION AND ROLE MODELING MORE IMPORTANT THAN PUNISHMENT IN DISCIPLINING CHILDREN?

Many children steal, cheat, and lie when they believe that the chances of getting caught, and hence punished, are slim, because they haven't learned to value honesty. A 2008 survey of almost 30,000 high school students, conducted by the Center for Youth Ethics at the Josephson Institute in Los Angeles, found that 30 percent stole from a store within the past year, 64 percent cheated on a test during the past year, and 82 percent lied to a parent about something significant during the past year.[12] Despite the high incidences of such responses, 93 percent of the students said that they were satisfied with their personal ethics and character, and 77 percent affirmed that "when it comes to doing what is right, I am better than most I know." These statistics make it clear that a large portion of parents have not been successful in teaching children to value honesty.

Punishment for being dishonest doesn't teach children to value honesty, it only teaches them to avoid being dishonest when there is a good chance that they will be caught and therefore punished. Children learn to value honesty when parents take the time to explain why it is important to be honest and why dishonesty is undesirable. For example, parents need to explain why people will be respected by others if they are honest but not if they are dishonest, and how dishonest actions negatively affect others. Children's books and real or made-up stories can help parents teach values like honesty.

Children also learn to value honesty by having their parents set a good example. It is important that they see their parents being honest, especially in situations where the parents will likely not get caught in dishonesty, such as keeping excess change that a store clerk has given them. Parents also need to avoid saying things that are not true, such as "Tell the caller that I'm not at home" or, to a child at the doctor's, "This injection will not hurt." By also keeping their commitments to their children, such as showing up when they say they will or accurately informing children how long something will take, such as shopping for groceries, they are also setting a good example.

Another way children learn to value honesty is by how their parents handle their acknowledgment of doing something wrong, such as breaking something that no one observed them break. If they are harshly punished for breaking an item and not complimented for their honesty in reporting that they broke it, they are much less likely to come to value honesty and will likely learn that dishonesty has its advantages. If, on the other hand, parents strongly communicate how proud they are that the child told the truth, and then either don't punish the child's misdeed or administer a mild punishment or one that the child agrees is fair, honesty will come to be valued.

Young children who are harshly punished for not obeying rules, but who rarely have had discussions with their parents about the reasons for various rules, will likely just blindly obey whatever rules the parents have put in place and have limited ability to think and reason about the rules. Most parents have a rule that their children should never speak with strangers. If the parents have not taken the time to explain why speaking to strangers is to be avoided, and to also explain that there are special circumstances when speaking with strangers might be necessary, their children will likely just blindly follow the rule, and this may have serious consequences. For example, children may be with a parent when the parent loses consciousness because of an injury or illness. In this case, blindly following the rule of not speaking with strangers might mean that the parent doesn't get the help that is needed. If parents help children understand the reasons behind the rules, children will be much more likely to want to follow them and will know when it makes sense not to follow them. They will also better understand what motivates their parents and will likely come to see them as a lot less restrictive and controlling.

So parents need to clearly communicate what their rules are and the logic or rationale behind them. They also need to teach by example and be sure that they follow their own rules.

How can the use of rewards dramatically reduce the need for administering punishments?

Reinforcement is a term psychologists use to refer to the use of rewards to strengthen behavior. Positive reinforcement is the addition of something desirable, such as a compliment or money. Negative reinforcement is the removal of something undesirable, such as chores or being grounded. Both positive and negative reinforcement increase the strength of behaviors that they follow. Both types of reinforcement are most effective when they immediately follow the behavior to be strengthened.

Since the goal of discipline is to teach, parents can use reinforcement to strengthen the values that their children are learning. By using reinforcement to increase the strength of desirable behaviors like sharing or telling the truth, undesirable behaviors like being selfish or lying are less likely to occur. However, it is of fundamental importance that in addition to rewarding desirable behavior, parents take the time to explain to children why certain behaviors are desired. The goal once again is to have children come to value things like honesty or generosity, not because they are rewarded by their parents, but because being honest or generous are desirable qualities to possess.

When a child isn't listening or obeying, parents often make the mistake of turning to punishment before trying other techniques, such as the use of reinforcement, to get the child to listen. When my daughter Andrea was three years old, instead of staying in her chair during dinner, she developed an annoying habit of roaming around the kitchen and adjacent rooms. After weeks of trying to change this behavior with persuasion, I saw little progress and was just about ready to turn to punishment when one day I said to her, "Andrea, how can I get you to remain in your chair during dinner?" To my great surprise, she answered, "How about a sticker chart, Dad?" Since my wife and I had only used a sticker chart with her once before during toilet training about a year previous, I certainly didn't expect this answer.

Right after dinner, we sat down together and made a big chart that Andrea decided should be placed on the refrigerator door. While she was decorating the chart, I asked her what reward she wanted when she completed filling up the chart with stickers. Her answer also surprised me, and was certainly nothing I would have ever considered. After some thought, she said, "I want my own garden." I said that would be fine, and we agreed that each night that she stayed in her chair throughout the entire dinnertime she would earn one sticker. The chart we made had spaces for fifteen stickers, and once the chart was filled she knew I would begin to work on preparing the ground so she could plant a small garden. It was late spring, so luckily her reward for filling the chart could occur in a timely manner. The next day, we made a special trip to a store so she could purchase new and interesting stickers to go on her chart. This system worked extremely well. The roaming behavior promptly ended, and by the start of summer she had planted her own garden. I could have employed punishment to teach her to stay in her chair, but obviously the experience for both of us would have been unpleasant, and I doubt it would have worked nearly as well. By the time she had completed the chart, she had already acquired the habit of remaining at the dinner table, and roaming didn't become a problem again.

Sticker charts are often used to help young children become toilet trained (only when they are developmentally ready, I would hope), but they can be used to alter any behavior. When properly employed, they work quite well. The most important thing to keep in mind when setting up a sticker chart is to involve the child as much as possible. That includes having the child help make the chart, decide where the chart will be placed, select the stickers that will go on the chart, and select the reward that will be given once the chart is filled with stickers. Parents, of course, can veto any unreasonable reward the child may select.

It is very difficult for young children to cooperate on long car trips. They get bored easily and often turn to tormenting each other as a form of amusement. While this is normal behavior, it is behavior that parents find most unpleasant. In an attempt to stop the tormenting, parents typically threaten to punish any fighting that occurs. However, a more effective procedure is for parents to use rewards as an incentive to cooperate.

When my daughters were five and nine years of age, we took a five-week car trip from our home in the western part of New York state to visit some of the national parks in the western United States. Knowing that being cooperative during long boring days spent in the car would not be easy for young children, I decided to use an incentive system (instead of a punitive system) to encourage cooperation. In the glove compartment of the car, I placed one sealed envelope for each long driving day. Inside each envelope was a piece of paper on which was written the name of a reward that my daughters could earn if they were cooperative throughout the day. I kept the contents of the envelopes secret. Rewards included things like selecting where we would eat dinner, purchasing souvenirs, or getting to go to an amusement park. Because it is normal for young children to argue and fight in this type of confined situation, I told them that they were allowed two warnings each day. If more than two incidences of "fighting" took place, they would lose the opportunity to open an envelope that day.

The system worked even better than I had expected. Not only were they extremely cooperative, but they were upset when we finally reached the first national park where we were going to stay for five days. Upon arriving at that park, I happily announced that for the next five days, they wouldn't have to spend hours riding in the car. After I said that, I noticed that my youngest daughter looked like she was about ready to cry. When I said, "Andrea, what's wrong?" she answered, "Dad, does that mean that we don't get to open any envelopes for the next five days?" Some other people, including my neighbors who traveled from New York to Alaska by car, have successfully used this incentive system. These examples illustrate that rewards can work extremely well in stopping misbehavior behavior while reducing or eliminating the need for punishment.

Because tangible rewards can weaken intrinsic motivation (the enjoyment inherent in a task or activity), it is best for parents to try to use non-tangible rewards, such as praise, to strengthen things like learning that ideally we would want children to find inherently interesting. The weakening effect of tangible rewards is greatest when the rewards are anticipated. A common but questionable practice that many parents employ is rewarding good performance in school with toys or money. Some parents let their children know ahead of time that they can earn a tangible reward by getting high grades. Often a specific dollar amount is designated for each high grade, for example $10 for every A and $5 for every B. While this strategy is likely to motivate children to work hard in school, they will primarily be doing so in order to get money, and their intrinsic motivation to learn will be reduced in the process. They will come to see the money as the benefit of learning, rather than the knowledge gained. The famous old fable about the Jewish tailor illustrates this point.[13]

In a little southern town where the Klan was riding again, a Jewish tailor had the temerity to open his little shop on the main street. To drive him out of the town, the Kleagle of the Klan sent a gang of little ragamuffins to annoy him. Day after day, they stood at the entrance of his shop. "Jew! Jew!" they hooted at him. The situation looked serious for the tailor. He took the matter so much to heart that he began to brood and spent sleepless nights over it. Finally, out of desperation, he evolved a plan.

The following day, when the little hoodlums came to jeer at him, he came to the door and said to them, "From today on, any boy who calls me 'Jew' will get a dime from me." Then he put his hand in his pocket and gave each boy a dime.

Delighted with their booty, the boys came back the following day and began to shrill, "Jew! Jew!" The tailor came out smiling. He put his hand in his pocket and gave each boy a nickel, saying, "A dime is too much—I can only afford a nickel today." The boys went away satisfied because, after all, a nickel was money too.

However, when they returned the next day to hoot at him, the tailor gave them only a penny each.

"Why do we get only a penny today?" they yelled.

"That's all I can afford."

"But two days ago you gave us a dime, and yesterday we got a nickel. It's not fair, mister."

"Take it or leave it. That's all you're going to get!"

"Do you think we're going to call you 'Jew' for one lousy penny?"

"So don't!"

And they didn't.

At first, without any compensation, the children enjoyed tormenting the tailor. But once they were paid to do so, their intrinsic motivation to torment was lost. So what they originally did just for fun, they were no longer willing to do unless they received money. Based on this old Jewish tailor fable and research studies done by Edward Deci and his colleagues on intrinsic motivation, to preserve intrinsic motivation, parents should primarily use non-tangible rewards, such as praise or spending time doing an activity that their child enjoys, to help teach desirable behaviors.[14] However, there may be times when intrinsic motivation is low to start with (e.g., children sitting quietly in a car on a long trip, as per the example above) and non-tangible rewards would likely be insufficient to alter behavior. In those cases, parents may decide as I did to use tangible rewards as a way to encourage desirable behavior.

WHAT ROLE SHOULD PUNISHMENT PLAY IN DISCIPLINE?

As already discussed, good communication is of fundamental importance in helping children understand rules and the rationale behind them. This, along with role modeling, enables children to acquire values to guide their behavior. Patience is also required on the part of parents, especially when dealing with younger children. Explaining things several times is often necessary.

When a rule is broken for the first time, a good starting point is to ask the child to go over the rule and the rationale behind it (why it is important that the rule be followed). This is often all that is needed to eliminate future misbehavior. However, there are times when children understand a rule and the rationale behind it but still choose to violate. Breaking rules is common during childhood and should not be considered abnormal—but it should also not be ignored.

Even though it is against the rules, siblings may fight with each other, or an older child may break curfew. Should this occur, parents may need to resort to punishment to correct the misbehavior, but they should first try other teaching techniques, because the aim is to get the child to come to the conclusion that the rule is reasonable and one that should be followed because it is the correct thing to do. For example, the goal should be to get siblings to not fight because they believe fighting is wrong, not because they fear suffering a huge penalty if they fight. Or the goal should be to get a child to adhere to a curfew because the child understands safety issues that may be involved and the important role that sleep plays in health and cognitive performance.

If other approaches fail—such as the parents writing a letter to their child carefully explaining why they are deeply concerned about the behavior, or having another person, such as a relative, friend, or minister talk with the child—the parents should resort to using either reinforcement or punishment to try to correct any repeated misbehavior. Because a reinforcement/incentive system is much more pleasant for parents to administer and for children to experience than a punishment system, it would make sense to try that first. An incentive system would involve the parents offering a reward if a rule, such as not fighting or keeping to a curfew, is followed.

If an incentive system fails to work, parents must resort to the use of punishment to try to eliminate the misbehavior. In doing so, they should remember that the goal in choosing a punishment should be to clearly communicate that breaking the rule is a very serious matter and to motivate the child to spend some time thinking about the misbehavior. The purpose of the punishment should not be to inflict misery or fear. Therefore, the punishment chosen should not be too harsh (unless the rule continues to be repeatedly violated, in which case progressively more severe punishments may be needed). Angry parents should not impose a punishment immediately, because in the heat of the moment the punishment chosen may be too severe. They should calm down first. One option is to discuss with the child what a suitable punishment should be. Ideally, a reasonable punishment will be agreed upon; if not, since the parents are in charge, they should inform the child what the punishment will be.

There are two categories of punishments to select from, positive punishments and negative punishments. Positive punishments are things that are added to the situation that the child dislikes, such as additional chores; negative punishments are things that are taken away that the child likes, such as an allowance. Sometimes parents don't realize that something they are doing that they view as punishment may actually be experienced by their child as reinforcement. For example, when parents scold a child, they do so because they believe scolding to be a mild form of positive punishment, which will reduce the chance of the misbehavior occurring as frequently. However, if the child craves parental attention, the scolding may actually be experienced by the child as positive reinforcement, and actually increase the chances of the misbehavior occurring again. In situations like this, it is often more effective for the parent to ignore the misbehavior if it is relatively minor and not reward the child with "negative" attention.

Like reinforcement, punishment is most effective if it is administered immediately following the behavior to be changed. Whenever possible, the punishment should be related to the "crime." For example, breaking a curfew might be punished by requiring the child to come home earlier next time they are out, rather than doing something totally unrelated like taking away the child's allowance. Fighting between siblings might be punished by requiring the siblings to stay in separate rooms for a period of time. Running out into the road to retrieve a ball without looking might be punished by requiring the child to play inside the house for a few days.

Parents should only resort to using punishment for discipline problems that they consider to be very serious. In other words, parents should pick their battles and not come down hard on minor misbehaviors. Children who are frequently punished don't like it, but they do get used to it, and as a result its impact weakens over time. Also, frequently punished children will likely come to see themselves as bad. This, of course, lowers self-esteem. So it is important to communicate that the behavior that is being punished is what is unacceptable or bad, not the child. A related issue is the words parents choose in correcting minor misbehaviors that don't warrant punishment. Parent often tell children what *not* to do instead of what *to* do. They often say to children, "Don't do that" or "Stop doing that." Instead, they should focus on what they would prefer the child to do. Instead of saying "Stop running," a parent might say "Please walk"; instead of saying "Stop screaming and shouting," a parent might say "Please use your quiet voice." If parents do this, children are less likely to feel that they are always being caught in bad behavior, which as mentioned isn't good for their self-esteem.

Remember, punishment should be used to let children know that the misbehavior is serious and to encourage them to think about their misbehavior. If children are always getting punished, they will have trouble determining if this time they are being punished for something minor or for something serious. Children who are used to getting punished are also much less likely to spend time thinking about their misbehavior; they just take their punishment and get on with their lives with little reflection. They might think that since they never seem to be able to avoid being punished, why should they even bother to try to contemplate what they did that was wrong?

It is important not to let serious misbehavior go on for very long. If all approaches to discipline fail, including punishment, and serious misbehavior continues, then it is time to seek professional help from a psychologist who specializes in working with children.

WHY SHOULD SPANKING NEVER BE USED AS A FORM OF DISCIPLINE?

Most adults believe that since they were spanked as children and they turned out okay, that spanking is a good parenting technique to employ. However, in order to decide if spanking really is a good technique, we need to have comparison studies of children who were spanked with those who were not. To use an analogy, when it comes to lung cancer, about 86 percent of smokers turn out okay (that is, only about 14 percent of smokers develop lung cancer).[15] However, in order to decide if smoking is a risk factor for developing lung cancer, we needed comparison studies of adults who smoked and those who did not. Such studies have found that only about 1.4 percent of non-smokers develop lung cancer. Therefore, although most smokers turn out okay (at least when it comes to developing lung cancer, but of course there are other health risks), smoking still increases by about ten times the likelihood of developing lung cancer. Using the same logic, although it is true that most people who were spanked turned out okay, spanking isn't necessarily a good discipline technique. In fact, comparison studies find that it is a poor technique. Parents who use other forms of discipline have better behaved children than parents who employ spanking.[16]

Parents should employ the best teaching techniques to help their children understand the rationale behind rules and acquire a set of guiding values. Spanking isn't one of those techniques, since its focus is on stopping behavior and not on teaching why it is wrong to engage in a behavior or the effects misbehavior has on others. It is also difficult for a spanked child who is distressed to be able to pay attention and learn what a parent is trying to teach, as stress produces brain changes that interfere with learning.[17]

Another reason to avoid spanking is that learning should be fun, not painful. When adults look back upon their education, they typically recall learning the most in the courses that they enjoyed attending, not the courses they feared attending.

We naturally try to be close to those who are nice to us and distance ourselves from those who hurt us. Since spanking hurts, we shouldn't be surprised that it weakens the bond between child and parent. The weaker the child-parent bond, the lower the likelihood that the child will want to do things to please the parents. If the spanking is frequent and/or severe, the child will come to fear and resent the parent(s) doing the spanking and be more likely to become anxious and depressed.[18] As a way of getting back at the parent(s), the child may become defiant, act out, and rebel, especially when he/she gets older. There is also data to show that those who were spanked as children have an increased probability of ending up in abusive relationships. They have learned that physical force is an acceptable way to control others, and since they experienced love and pain mixed together during childhood, they accept this as normal.[19]

Spanking children is typically also associated with other problems, including:

Aggressive Behavior: Spanked children are more likely to be defiant, have temper tantrums, and lash out physically against others.[20]

Physical Abuse: Parents who spank, and especially those who hit with objects, are more likely to physically abuse their children.[21]

Lower Intelligence: Spanking slows cognitive development. The children of parents who spank have a 2.8-5.0 point lower IQ score.[22]

Criminal Behavior: Spanking increases the risk of childhood delinquency and adult criminal behavior.[23]

Sexual Problems: Children who were spanked are more likely to verbally and physically coerce a dating partner into having sex, are twice as likely to have unprotected premarital sex, and almost twice as likely to have masochistic sex.[24]

In August of 2009, following an extensive review of the scientific literature on corporal punishment (punishment that inflicts pain), the Family Services Division of the American Psychological Association (APA) concluded that "parents and caregivers should reduce and potentially eliminate their use of any physical punishment as a disciplinary measure."[25] The review team of fifteen experts in child development and psychology found correlations between the use of physical punishment and an increase in childhood anxiety and depression, an increase in behavioral problems including aggression, and impaired cognitive development.

Without realizing it, parents who spank are teaching their children that it is okay for a more powerful person to use physical force to control a less powerful person. This is a terrible lesson to be teaching children and helps to explain the problematic pattern of sexual behavior mentioned above. Not surprisingly, children who are frequently spanked tend to see themselves as bad and often develop low self-esteem. They are also more likely to become bullies and use force to intimidate less powerful children.[26] Using force to control other children is a way to boost their self-esteem. If all children grew up experiencing only nonviolent means of discipline, they would be much less likely to try to solve problems using physical force, and the world we live in would be a lot less violent.

In summary, spanking is to be avoided because it isn't a very effective teaching technique, it weakens the child-parent bond, and it is associated with many undesirable side effects—plus it role-models the use of physical force to control another person.

WHAT ROLE CAN NATURAL AND LOGICAL CONSEQUENCES PLAY IN HELPING TO DISCIPLINE CHILDREN?

All too often, parents are impatient; rather than letting things take their own natural course, they intervene. Most often, the intervention involves either nagging or threatening the child with punishment. Less frequently, parents intervene with a bribe (a reinforcement incentive). For example, children often have trouble getting ready for school on their own. Rather than taking steps to encourage them to be self-directed and figure out a way to get ready on time by themselves, parents tend to take on this responsibility. The parents may repeatedly wake the children up or gather their things together for them, for fear that they might either miss the school bus or arrive late if they walk to school or are transported by car. The parents may also threaten the children with punishment, perhaps by saying each time that they are not ready by a specific time they will miss an hour of TV viewing. Another tactic is to bribe the child with an incentive, perhaps promising to buy some desired item if, for an entire week, they get ready on time. Of course, many parents combine nagging with either punishment or bribes.

Another option to change the tardy behavior is to allow natural consequences to take place. Assuming that there is a history of the parents taking on the responsibility of getting their children ready on time, a good place to start the change process is for the parents to have a discussion with the child about responsibility. During the discussion the parents can explain why it is important for people to learn how to manage their own affairs, and that from now on it is the child's responsibility to get ready on time. The parent must then forget about nagging, punishing, or bribing, and just let natural consequences occur. If a child arrives late to school, natural consequences would include whatever penalty (punishment) the school imposes, and most likely some embarrassment. If a school bus is involved, the child should be warned that if the bus is missed, other natural consequences will come into play. The child will need to figure out some other way to get to school, possibly by using allowance money to pay for a taxi; if safety isn't a concern, walking to school might be another option.

Because sometimes it takes natural consequences a long time to impact behavior, logical consequences can be used to speed up the process. For example, most children go through a period of time when they dislike taking showers or baths. Parents often find themselves nagging or threatening the child to get them to stay clean. Parents should of course explain to the child that when they don't bathe regularly they will develop body odor and skin rashes, and other people won't want to be around them. If the discussion doesn't change the behavior, then given enough time, natural consequences most likely would alter the behavior (other people would eventually avoid the child). However, using logical consequences can greatly speed up the process. One logical consequence would be for family members to avoid being in close proximity to the "smelly" child. For example, even before they actually smell bad, the child may be told that he/she is no longer welcome at the dinner table and must eat alone some distance away. Another logical consequence would be to refuse to be in a confined space with the child, and hence refuse to transport the child to events or allow the child to go on family outings that involve car transport.

While natural and logical consequences function much like punishment, reducing the probability of an undesirable behavior continuing, they are often interpreted differently by the child. For example, if a child comes home late for dinner, a natural consequence would be for the child to have to prepare food and eat it alone. Most children don't enjoy doing that, but they understand it and tend to see it as fair. On the other hand, if the parents decide to dock a week's allowance as punishment for being late for dinner, the child is more likely to see that as unfair. The child-parent relationship tends to be better if natural and logical consequences are used instead of more traditional punishments.

When issues of safety are involved, waiting for natural consequences to alter a child's behavior amounts to neglectful parenting. For example, if parents have explained the importance of wearing a bicycle helmet and the child is observed riding without one, they should not allow the child to experience a head injury as a way to teach bicycle safety. In that case, imposing a logical consequence would be appropriate, such as taking away bicycle privileges for a period of time. It is also important that parents are good role models and always wear a helmet even if they aren't required to do so by law.

WHY IS BEING CONSISTENT IMPORTANT WHEN DISCIPLINING CHILDREN?

Parents need to consistently give children the same messages. If children are only encouraged to be well-behaved when guests are present, they will not learn to value being well-behaved, they will just learn to be well-behaved in certain situations in order to avoid punishment, or possibly to receive a reward. If parents communicate that it is important to be polite to adults but not to other people, children will not truly learn to value politeness.

It's normal for children to test limits—to see what they truly can and cannot get away with. This is part of the process of establishing autonomy. This means that parents will need to consistently follow polices that they have put in place if their children are to learn appropriate values. This includes being sure that consequences for policy violations are routinely applied. Many parents are more inconsistent in applying consequences than they realize. Take temper tantrums for example. Most parents occasionally give in to children (thus rewarding the tantrum behavior) because they want to avoid the embarrassment that occurs when a child "makes a scene" in public or at a family holiday get-together. Any behavior, including temper tantrums, that is infrequently rewarded will be very hard to eliminate. Psychologists refer to this as the partial reinforcement effect: behaviors that are reinforced part of the time are very resistant to extinction. In addition to the desire to avoid embarrassment, reasons for inconsistent follow-through include parents being too tired or one parent not truly believing in a rule.

In most cases, if parents are able to consistently ignore temper tantrums, the temper tantrums will stop. If tantrums persist, a form of punishment known as time-out can be helpful. Time-out involves removing the child from the environment where the inappropriate behavior occurred and placing the child in a quiet space without any toys, games, or other distractions. This both punishes the inappropriate behavior by taking the child away from the "action" and gives the child time to calm down and think about the misbehavior. As a rule of thumb, for each year of age the child should remain in time-out for one to two minutes. At the end of the time-out period, the parents should discuss the incident with the child to be sure that the child understands why the time-out was necessary and how such a punishment might be avoided in the future.

Inconsistency also leads to slower learning. For example, if parents have a rule that no physical fighting between siblings is allowed, they have to be sure that they don't let some fights go "unrecognized." If they do, the children will be a lot slower to learn to follow the rule and to understand that the parents really mean what they say. It can also be initially confusing to children when there are two parents in the home and one lets certain rule violations go unnoticed and the other doesn't. Eventually, the children will figure out what each parent will let them get away with. In this case, the children are simply learning how to avoid punishment and are less likely to learn to get along with each other and appreciate that fighting is wrong.

Parents also need to consistently set a good example. If they don't want their children to use foul language, they have to be careful not to slip up and occasionally curse. Slipping up will teach children that foul language is okay in certain situations. If parents hope to teach the value of honesty, they need to avoid even occasionally being dishonest. Doing so will indirectly teach children that honesty isn't always the best policy, and that dishonestly is okay in certain situations. This of course means that parents need to carefully monitor their own behavior at all times. They should acknowledge any slip ups, and where appropriate apologize to their children.

How can reminders help with discipline?

When parents are aware that in certain situations their children tend to misbehave, they should be sure to remind the children ahead of time just what behavior is expected. If possible, they should also try to avoid placing the child in difficult situations if the child is tired or hungry. For example, many children have trouble behaving well in supermarkets. They see many things on the shelves that they find attractive, and they become upset when they are told that they can't have them. If parents go the supermarket with well-rested and well-fed children, and they take time before entering the store to remind children what is expected, the children will generally behave much better. Part of the discussion should include setting limits, such as telling children that good cooperation will be rewarded with each child getting to pick out one box of cereal or one dessert item. Parents should also discuss what will happen if good cooperation doesn't take place. For example, the children might be told that if they misbehave, the visit to the store will promptly end, and the parents will not purchase any items that they have selected. Should misbehavior take place, it is important that the parents keep their word, even if it means leaving the store without all of the items they had planned to purchase.

Another situation that is often difficult for children is visits to the homes of other people, especially those who don't have any children. Many parents childproof their own home, and so the children can play with most anything that they can see and can reach. This of course isn't typically the case in other homes where children are not normally present. So, in preparation for such visits, children should be well-rested and not hungry, and they should be told to ask if it is okay before touching anything. Part of the discussion should include the reason for this, such as some of the things in the house about to be visited are treasured items that can be easily broken and may be irreplaceable.

WHY IS IT IMPORTANT FOR PARENTS TO UNDERSTAND A VARIETY OF DIFFERENT PARENTING TECHNIQUES AND BE WILLING TO EMPLOY THEM?

After many unsuccessful attempts to eliminate a child's misbehavior through discussion, parents may "give up" and think that they just have a "problem child" or a "rotten kid." They often place blame for the misbehavior on the child instead of on their parenting techniques. They often resort to punishing the child for the misbehavior rather than trying other techniques to correct the misbehavior. This is counterproductive, because even if the problem behavior is not related to their parenting—for example, they have a child who has a biologically based problem like attention deficit hyperactivity disorder (ADHD) or a learning disability (LD)—it is best for the parents to continue to try new approaches to deal with the problem. Let me use a personal example to illustrate this.

When my oldest daughter was almost eleven years old, she began to develop the habit of leaving important things, such as school reports, for the last minute. My concern was not her grades, which were always excellent, but the fact that waiting till the last minute to do important things was a bad habit to develop, one that would eventually not serve her well. Over the course of several months, I had numerous discussions with her about this, including a few heated ones, but her procrastination continued. Since the discussion strategy I was using was ineffective, I was tempted to view the problem as hers, and either give up (and hope that natural consequences would eventually reduce her procrastination) or employ punishment, rather than to view the problem as mine and try to find another approach to solving it. I was reluctant to use punishment to control her procrastination because I wanted her to be self-directed. I knew if I did resort to punishment, she would likely comply just to avoid being punished, when what I really wanted was for her to come to value doing important things in a timely manner.

Since neither giving up nor resorting to punishment appealed to me, I racked my brain and eventually came up with a different approach. I wrote her a letter, very carefully expressing how I felt about our heated discussions and guessing how she felt about my continual "harassment" and the power struggle that we were in. The letter allowed me to express my thoughts and feelings without interruption, which a conversation doesn't typically allow, and it enabled my daughter to more fully understand why I thought procrastination was a problem. Since she had never before received a letter from me, this one received her full attention. The letter was successful in reducing her procrastination, but the important point here is that when one parenting strategy isn't working, rather than sticking to it or giving up, it is best to try a different approach, and if possible one that doesn't involve punishment.

SUMMARY

The primary goal of discipline should be to teach children a set of values so they can become self-directed and caring people. This can best be accomplished by parents taking the time to careful explain to children the reasons why they would like them to behave in certain ways and modeling the behaviors they would like their child to engage in. When it comes to teaching values and to raising successful children, an authoritative parenting style works best. Rewards and punishments, while a lot less important than good communication and leading by example, also have a place in discipline. However, spanking as a form of punishment should be avoided, because it isn't a very effective technique for teaching values, and it is associated with many serious side effects. Also, children who are spanked behave more poorly than children who have been raised using other discipline techniques.

Parents should try to use natural and logical consequences to change behavior, because children see those forms of punishment as fairer than other forms of punishment. Parents should strive to be consistent when disciplining their children and remind their children of the behaviors that they expect. Finally, if one discipline technique isn't working, parents should be flexible and creative in finding others.

Chapter 5
Divorce and Family Configurations

- What are the benefits of children spending their entire childhood with the same set of parents?
- How does divorce impact children?
- If parents decide to get divorced, how should they go about telling their children?
- How can parents minimize the negative impact that divorce typically has on children?
- Why does even a "good" divorce force children to grow up very quickly?
- Under what circumstances do children benefit from divorce?
- How do children raised by homosexual parents compare to children raised by heterosexual parents?
- How do children raised by grandparents compare to children raised by nongrandparents?
- What special challenges do adoptive parents face?

What are the benefits of children spending their entire childhood with the same set of parents?

Fifty years ago, about 5 percent of children were born to unwed parents and about 25 percent of marriages ended in divorce. That meant that the majority of children had the benefit of living with and being raised by both of their biological parents. Today things are very different.

Currently, about 40 percent of children are born to unwed parents and about 45 percent of current marriages are expected to end in divorce.[1, 2] As a result, the majority of children now spend at least part of their childhood living with and being raised by a single parent, a single parent and a stepparent, adoptive parents, or one or two grandparents. This certainly isn't the ideal situation for children or for parents.

As mentioned in the first two chapters of this book, raising a child is an awesome responsibility that requires an ever-changing skill set. Even under the best of circumstances, when one set of parents is there for the duration, there are many challenges. Raising a child alone, or for part of the time with a stepparent, adds many additional stresses for all family members.

Compared to children growing up in single-parent families, children growing up with two continuously married parents are less likely to experience a wide range of cognitive problems (e.g., lower school grades and lower scores on standardized tests), emotional problems (e.g., aggressive behavior, low self-esteem, and depression), and social problems (e.g., smaller number of close friends, limited social support from peers). This is true not only during childhood, but also in adulthood.[3,4] In addition, children in divorced families typically don't feel as emotionally close to their parents as children from intact families. This is particularly true if their parents have a high-conflict relationship. It should also be pointed out that stresses related to marital disruption can impair the functioning of the immune system and result in increased health problems.[5]

Like children of divorce, children born outside of marriage have more problems on average. As Judith S. Wallerstein and Sandra Blakeslee write in *Second Chances: Men, Women and Children a Decade After Divorce*, "Compared with children who grow up in stable, two-parent families, children born outside marriage reach adulthood with less education, earn less income, have lower occupational status, are more likely to be idle (that is, not employed and not in school), are more likely to have a nonmarital birth (among daughters), have more troubled marriages, experience higher rates of divorce, and report more symptoms of depression."[6] Children living in a single-parent home that is the result of the death of one parent are at risk for a number of problems, including depression and dropping out of school, but overall not as much at risk as children of divorce or children resulting from out-of-wedlock births.

Loss of parental contact is a frequent side-effect of divorce. Wallerstein and Blakeslee found that before divorce, stay-at-home mothers had forty-five hours of contact per week with their children; after divorce, only eleven hours.[7] Before divorce, employed mothers in two-parent families had twenty-five hours per week of contact with their children; after divorce, just five-and-a-half hours. Before divorce, employed fathers in two-parent families had twenty hours of contact per week; after divorce, just two hours. Single parents who have sole custody of their children have all or most of the responsibilities associated with raising them and taking care of a household. Without having someone to share all of this, it is obvious that on average their children would receive a lot less parental time than children who are being raised by two people.

Single parents often also struggle financially, which means that many have to work more than one job or put in overtime. In addition, they often invest some time in dating. This all contributes to their children receiving less parental time. Besides having less time to parent, single parents often lack the opportunity to consult with someone who knows their child well when parenting issues develop. This can add to their stress level, since two heads are typically better than one at solving problems. The additional economic and workload stress experienced by single parents helps to explain why, as a group, the quality of parenting that they provide is poorer.[8, 9] Single parents tend to have fewer rules and provide less supervision.[10, 11] According to *Growing Up With a Single Parent: What Hurts, What Helps*, "Compared with teenagers of similar backgrounds, who grew up with both parents at home, adolescents who have lived apart from one of their parents during some period of childhood are twice as likely to drop out of high school, twice as likely to have a child before age twenty, and one and a half times more likely to be "idle"—out of school and out of work—in their late teens and early twenties."[12]

According to the US Census, in 2006, 8.1 percent of children under the age of eighteen who resided in two-parent families lived below the poverty level, compared to 42 percent of children who lived in single-parent families headed by women and 20.3 percent of children who lived in single-parent families headed by men.[13] While the lack of money certainly doesn't have to lead to a poorer parenting outcome, it often does. Poor people tend to receive lower-quality prenatal and early postnatal care. They also need to be more focused on the cost of child-care than on its quality. As poor children get older, they are much more likely to be left unsupervised and are less likely to participate in after-school activities that aren't free. Parents may not be able to provide school supplies and a home computer. Poor families also tend to live in less desirable neighborhoods with poorer schools, higher crime rates, and fewer community services. These economic factors make it much more difficult for poor children to succeed, regardless of whether they live in a single-parent or dual-parent home.

Some of the effects of being raised by a single parent appear to be positive. Research has consistently shown that children from divorced families mature more rapidly, are more independent, and exhibit less stereotypical sex-type behavior.[14] These differences are the result of children of divorce being on their own more than children from intact marriages and observing their custodial parent engaging in more cross-gender behaviors. However, "forced" maturity and independence can rob children of part of their childhood. When children of divorce look back on their childhood, they often report that carefree play existed before but not after their parents' divorce.[14]

Whether a child is raised by one biological parent or by one biological parent and one stepparent, one important factor is the role that the nonresident biological parent plays, assuming that both biological parents are alive. If the nonresident biological parent is closely involved in the children's lives, they are likely to do better academically and experience fewer emotional and conduct problems. If the nonresident parent is not involved in the children's life, then at some point in time the children will wonder why that is the case. Regardless of the actual reason, it is common for children to experience feelings of abandonment, especially if they lived with both biological parents for a period of time before the divorce or separation. Wallerstein and Blakeslee found that ten years post-divorce, about 75 percent of children felt rejected by their noncustodial parent.[15] Children often experience a considerable amount of anger and jealousy if the nonresident biological parent remarries and has children with a new partner or invests time and resources into a new partner's children. Children will also experience some degree of insecurity. After all, if they can't count on both of their biological parents being there for them, what can they count on? Because children typically want to protect their divorced parents from further agony, their feelings of anger, jealousy, and insecurity will often be held inside and not shared.

If both biological parents are involved in their children's lives, then issues of abandonment and insecurity will be reduced, but other issues may develop if a stepparent enters the picture. Feelings of resentment and jealousy are quite common. Initially, the stepparent may be viewed as an intruder whose relationship with the biological parent takes up time that could have been spent with the children. Out of allegiance to the nonresident biological parent, who is usually the father, the children may resist developing a relationship with the new stepparent, usually a stepfather. However, should their resident biological parent, usually their mother, enter into a relationship with a partner of the same sex (another woman), allegiance to the nonresident biological parent (usually the father) should become much less of an issue, because it will not appear to the children that their nonresident biological parent is being "replaced," and the children will typically more easily establish a relationship with their parent's new homosexual partner. This is especially true if the children are young. Older children are likely to struggle a bit because of homophobia and/or fear of what peers might say.

If the stepparent has children, the children of the blended family may not appreciate having to share their parents and their things. Also, children who are part of a blended family may resent the additional live-in parent, since now an additional adult will in part be "controlling" what they do, and they may not be happy with some of the rule and routine changes which will likely occur. The children may challenge the authority of the new stepparent. Finally, once one parent remarries, the children's hope sadly ends that their biological parents will reconcile and one day remarry and make the family whole again.

According to a report in the *Journal of Marriage and Family*, "Children raised in step-and single-parent families have, on average, poorer academic, psychological, and behavioral outcomes than children raised in simple two parent families, resulting in lower educational and socioeconomic attainment and an increased likelihood of delinquent behavior, teen pregnancy, school dropout, and substance abuse."[16]

There are, of course, potential benefits to being part of a blended family, but realizing them generally takes time. After about five to seven years, the stress level of a stepfamily matches the stress level of an intact family.[17] Having two adults raising children in one household is considerably less expensive than maintaining two households. This increases the chances that at least some of the blended-family members will be living in a better situation, possibly attending better schools and/or living in a safer neighborhood. With two parents to share both parenting and household responsibilities, the total amount of parental time that each child receives will likely increase. Now if parenting problems develop, each parent will have someone to consult with who knows the child well.

HOW DOES DIVORCE IMPACT CHILDREN?

According to E. Mavis Hetherington, a pioneer in the field of developmental psychology and expert on family relationships, about 25 percent of children continue to suffer social and psychological problems six years post-divorce, which of course means that about 75 percent appear to have adjusted well. However, only about 10 percent of children from intact families suffer comparable problems.[18] That means the likelihood of children of divorce experiencing adjustment problems is two-and-a-half times that of children from intact families. Hetherington also found that about 20 percent of children of divorce become poorly adjusted adults, compared to about 10 percent of children from intact families. Clearly, children of divorce have lived for a period of time with at least one discontented parent and likely witnessed some marital discord. Part of the poorer outcome that the children of divorce experience stems from spending time living in a less than ideal two-parent family situation, and part may be attributable to the effects of divorce. In the four years preceding parental separation, children develop behavior problems and perform more poorly on standardized reading and math tests. The greater the parental conflict during this time period, the greater the impact on the children's behavior and academic performance.[19]

In 1971, Judith Wallerstein began a 25-year longitudinal study on the impact of divorce. Before Wallerstein began to publish her research findings, most psychologists believed that after a couple of years children would have largely adjusted to their parents' divorce and that there would be few long-term effects. Unfortunately, that isn't what Wallerstein found. She and her colleagues found that divorce negatively impacts children for decades.

Wallerstein tracked 131 children from sixty families whose parents were in the process of getting a divorce. At the time of the divorce, most of the children were six to ten years of age, and they came from middle-class and upper middle-class families living in Marin County, California. In 1996, she added a matched comparison group of forty-three children who lived in the same area but whose parents remained married.

Wallerstein found that the children of divorce were more aggressive and more depressed, had more problems with peers and more learning difficulties, were sexually active at an earlier age, were more likely to use drugs and alcohol, and were much more likely to be referred to a psychologist. She also found that the most significant impact of divorce occurred when the children became young adults and struggled with establishing trusting and stable long-term romantic relationships. As Wallerstein put it, young adults "have the fear that disaster was always waiting to strike without warning."[20] They probably believe that if their family fell apart, often with little warning, then so can most anything else, including their romantic relationships.

In a national study of 1,500 young adults, Elizabeth Marquardt found that 44 percent of grown children whose parents had divorced before the children reached the age of fourteen said that after the divorce, "I was alone a lot as a child," while only 14 percent of grown children from intact families felt alone as children.[21] Marquardt also found that 69 percent of children from intact families sought comfort from their families, while only 33 percent of children from divorced families sought comfort from their families. The children of divorce were more likely to seek comfort from siblings or peers or to comfort themselves. The majority (64 percent) of young adults of divorce indicated that they experienced stress in their family, compared with just 25 percent from intact families. Finally, and perhaps most significant, only one-third of the divorced sample strongly agreed with the statement "children were at the center of my family," compared to 63 percent of children from the intact family sample.

IF PARENTS DECIDE TO GET DIVORCED, HOW SHOULD THEY GO ABOUT TELLING THEIR CHILDREN?

Most divorces involve a tremendous amount of turmoil that affects all family members. In describing the situation, children are likely to say "we are getting a divorce" instead of "our parents are getting a divorce." That is because they see the divorce as the breakup of the family, not just the breakup of the marriage. While parents who are not getting along can see the benefits that a divorce will likely provide, children rarely can.[22] Most often their preference would be for the divorce not to take place. In many ways, it is the children who pay the greatest price for their parents not getting along and divorcing.

It is common for children to feel at least partially responsible for the breakup of the family. That is because they often observe their parents arguing about many things, including them. They often think that if they had been better behaved, their parents wouldn't have argued and fought as much, and might not have decided to get divorced and break up the family.

Telling children about an impending divorce is both stressful and challenging. Often parents are uncomfortable and want to avoid upsetting their children any more than is absolutely necessary, so they communicate as little as possible. That is a mistake. Since children are often not aware that their parents' marriage is struggling, they typically are caught off guard and confused by their parents' decision to end the marriage. Children need to understand that a decision as significant as getting a divorce is one that their parents take very seriously. Before telling the children, the parents should confer and agree on what will be said. Since it is best if the children have some time to adjust to the news while both parents can provide reassurance, the news should be delivered while both parents are still residing in the same house with their children. With all of the children present, and a large block of time available, both parents together should do the following:

Explain a little about why they have decided to get a divorce. At least communicate that things between them have not been going well for some time, and that even though they have tried hard to fix things they haven't been successful, and as a result they have decided to get divorced. The level of detail of the explanation will of course depend on the ages of the children. It is important to avoid the blame game in providing the explanation.

Repeatedly communicate that the children are in no way responsible for the divorce, and that nothing that they could have done would have prevented it from happening.

Make it clear that the parents are divorcing each other, not their children. The children need to be reassured that although their parents will no longer be living together, they both still plan to stay fully involved in their lives (unless the divorce stems from the fact that one of the parents put the children's health or safety at risk).

Explain how things will change for the children as a result of the divorce, including who will live where. Removing some of the uncertainly about what lies ahead will help to reduce the amount of stress children experience.

Encourage the children to ask questions and to express feelings, at the time the news is delivered and throughout the months and years ahead. If both parents are able to communicate the news without getting overly emotional, the children will feel more comfortable asking questions and expressing their feelings. Divorce has a traumatic and long-lasting impact on children. It is normal for them to feel many emotions, including shock, anger, sadness, resentment, confusion and anxiety. Some of these emotions stay with the children for decades and put a strain on the parent-child relationship. Adult children of divorced parents feel less affection for their parents, especially their fathers, and have less contact with both of their parents.[23] Pre-divorce marital discord is partially responsible for the emotional and physical distancing. If there was a high level of open pre-divorce parental conflict, then the children may also feel a sense of relief when they learn that their parents plan to divorce.

How can parents minimize the negative impact that divorce typically has on children?

Parents should make it clear that although things are not good now, the marriage was a success since it resulted in their parents' greatest joy, their children. At the same time, they should minimize the amount of parental conflict. When parents are at war with each other before, during, or following a divorce, children greatly suffer. Children should never be forced to choose a side during a conflict. High conflict emotionally distances children from their parents, and during and following a divorce it is extremely important that children feel close to both parents. Also, handling the divorce in an amicable manner provides the children with an example of healthy conflict resolution.

Children want to love both parents. It is very distressing for a child to hear negative things said about someone they love, especially coming from one of their parents. Therefore, one parent should never put down another parent in the children's presence. Also, children should feel free to say positive things about one parent in front of the other without feeling disloyal. On the other hand, one parent should not lie to cover up irresponsible behavior on the part of the other parent. Doing so will result in a loss of credibility, since children are likely to find out the truth or may already know it.

Following a divorce in which there is sole custody, typically over time there is a loss of contact with the nonresident parent. Usually it is the father who moves out of the house. Within two years post-divorce, only 25 percent of noncustodial fathers saw their children at least once a week, and six years post-divorce only 25 percent of noncustodial fathers saw their children once a year or more.[24] If a parent reduces or loses contact, the children will experience a sense of abandonment. They may also wonder if this is in part because there is something wrong with them—they don't deserve to be loved. Unfortunately, the loss of contact with one parent often also means that the children lose contact with family members from that side of the family. If possible, that should be avoided.

Unless the health and welfare of the children are at stake, it is very important that the children spend time with the nonresident parent. It is crucial for the nonresident parent to initially have daily contact with the children, either in person or by phone. If the parents are able to get along with each other, doing an occasional activity as an entire family, such celebrating birthdays or holidays together, is something that the children will greatly appreciate.

The interests of the children should always come first. Since the parents are the ones seeking the divorce, they should alter their lives in such a way as to limit the amount of disruption that their children experience. This would include both parents continuing to live close to each other so the children have easy access to them. The further a divorced parent lives from the children, the greater the likelihood of emotional disconnection. However, if a distant father frequently lets his children know that he cares and shows up for important events in their lives, positive relationships can be maintained.[25]

It is important for the children be consulted regarding the time that they will be scheduled to spend with each parent. Any schedule that gets worked out should be understood to be semi-flexible, so that the children don't miss out on important events because it's time to be with a parent who doesn't live close to a particular event.

Children should not be burdened with adult responsibilities because their parents decided to get a divorce. Although it isn't easy to avoid, parents should make an effort not to rush their children into growing up because of the divorce. Unless absolutely necessary, the children should not be given additional responsibilities related to the care of siblings or household chores. Children should not be pressured into replacing the "missing" parent. A mother should avoid making the son the man of the house. A father should avoid having his daughter replace the woman in his life. The children should not be leaned on for emotional support or expected to organize events, such as a parent's birthday celebration. When young adult children become caregivers and/or advisors to their divorcing parents, their own lives often get off track.

Parents should frequently communicate directly with each other and never use children as messengers. The children shouldn't be asked to communicate things like a change of plans or information about a late child-support check. Children should also never be used as bargaining chips by the parents and never interrogated to find out information about a former spouse.

It is important not to feel sorry for the children and relax rules or expectations. There is a lot of change and uncertainly associated with divorce; having rules and expectations remain consistent is reassuring to children. Parents should avoid trying to drown the sadness the children experience as a result of the divorce by doing things like giving them gifts. It is best if the children are allowed to experience and share their sadness, rather than try to cover it up. Parents who have infrequent contact with their children find it difficult not to lavish gifts on them, in part out of guilt, and in part because they want their limited time to be as positive as possible. "Disneyland Dads" not only lavish gifts, but they also spend most of their time with their children doing fun activities rather than providing real parenting. At first, children enjoy the fun and games, but over time they would prefer to have a real parent-child relationship instead.

Important people in the children's lives, such as relatives, teachers and coaches, should be notified about the divorce. Letting people who can provide support know about a difficult situation that a child is going though can be helpful for both the child and the people who interact with the child. Children clearly benefit by having an opportunity to speak with an adult when their parents are going through a divorce.

The parents should be very cautious about involving the children in their relationships with new romantic interests. The children have already suffered one loss and don't need to experience additional losses. They also might be upset when they see someone "taking" their mother's or father's place. Remarriage or blending families should be recognized as a very stressful time for children. Pressure should not be placed on them to accept the new stepparent or stepfamily. The parents should be patient and understand that acceptance will take time.

For the benefit of all family members, mediation by a neutral third party should be sought if there is high conflict following a divorce. Mediation has been shown to be a great stress-reducer and helps to decrease bickering and improve communication. Children are much better able to cope with divorce if their parents are able to get along civilly.

Parents should not hesitate to get professional help if serious adjustment problems are experienced by them or by their children. All family members find divorce to be extremely stressful. Both parents and children are likely to suffer some degree of sadness and anger at the breakup of the family. If any family member experiences depression, feels a high level of anxiety, or begins to seriously act out, professional help is warranted. In most cases, family therapy will work better than individual therapy.

WHY DOES EVEN A "GOOD" DIVORCE FORCE CHILDREN TO GROW UP VERY QUICKLY?

Compared to a bitter divorce, an amicable one where parents communicate with each other in a civil manner, have shared custody, and continue to coparent their children is highly desirable and makes life much easier for all family members. Nonetheless, there are some additional strains put on children no matter how well their divorced parents get along. For one thing, they now have two different residences to deal with. They need to more carefully keep track of their belongings, or they may find that when they are in one place the things they want are in the other place. How does a child feel fully at home in either residence if only some of their belongings are with them? Depending on how far apart the parents live, children may also need to develop two separate sets of friends. Celebrating holidays or other important occasions also can be complicated. Does Thanksgiving dinner get alternated from year to year, or is dinner eaten at one location and dessert at another? Compared to children from intact families, over twice as many children from divorced families consider the holidays to be stressful (36 percent vs. 15 percent).[26]

According to Elizabeth Marquardt, the task of marriage is for two adults to meld two differing worlds into one.[27] Parents who live together are more likely to compromise and have beliefs, values, and ways of living that are more alike than parents who live apart following a divorce. Divorced parents are more likely to drift apart in their views and lifestyles. Children of divorce who spend time with both parents are forced to make sense out of and bridge two very different worlds. Confronting their parents' differing values and beliefs can be both challenging and stressful, and causes them to formulate their own at an earlier age than children who live in a single residence with both of their parents. Marquardt found that 58 percent of the young adults of divorced families agreed with the statement, "I always felt like an adult, even when I was a kid," compared to 37 percent of a sample of children from intact homes.

UNDER WHAT CIRCUMSTANCES DO CHILDREN BENEFIT FROM DIVORCE?

High-conflict parental relationships that involve violence, addiction, frequent quarreling, and other serious problems take their toll on children.[28] Parents in high-conflict marriages tend to have children who are more anxious and experience stress-related headaches and stomachaches. Both the quality and quantity of their sleep is reduced, and they are more tired during the daytime and perform more poorly at school.[29] They have trouble controlling their anger and often act out. They also have lower self-esteem and an increased chance of becoming depressed and isolating themselves from their friends.

When divorces end high-conflict marriages, children fare better than children who remain in intact high-conflict families, especially if the divorce results in a reduction of the level of conflict and bitterness. When there is high parental conflict in an intact family, the children experience many of the same problems that are experienced by children of divorce, sometimes even more severely. Because of all of the energy devoted to arguing and fighting, parents involved in high-conflict relationships invest less energy in parenting and are less emotionally available to their children. As a result, children develop weaker bonds with both of their parents. They may also fail to learn interpersonal skills useful in conflict resolution. This contributes to the problems they experience when they establish intimate relationships. Compared to the children of divorced high-conflict marriages, children in intact high-conflict marriages have fewer friends, greater psychological distress and unhappiness, and poorer marriages as young adults.[30] Also, when high conflict continues post-divorce, father-child relationships are particularly jeopardized.[31] The number of behavior problems that children experience is highest if their high-conflict parents remain married, second highest if their high-conflict parents are divorced, third highest if their low-conflict parents get divorced, and lowest if their low-conflict parents remain married.[32]

HOW DO CHILDREN RAISED BY HOMOSEXUAL PARENTS COMPARE TO CHILDREN RAISED BY HETEROSEXUAL PARENTS?

About 40 percent of same-sex couples in the United States are raising children.[33] As of 2005, an estimated 270,313 of children in the United States were living in households headed by same-sex couples.[34]

In 2002, the American Academy of Pediatrics did a literature review on same-sex parents.[35] The review found that lesbian mothers are similar to heterosexual mothers on measures of self-esteem, anxiety, depression, parenting stress, and child-rearing practices. However, lesbian mothers were more concerned with providing a male role model for their children than divorced heterosexual mothers. The review also found that gay and heterosexual fathers are similar in many ways, but stated that "Compared with heterosexual fathers, gay fathers have been described to adhere to stricter disciplinary guidelines, to place greater emphasis on guidance and the development of cognitive skills, and to be more involved in their children's activities."

In 2004, Jennifer Wainwright and her colleagues looked at the psychosocial adjustment, school outcomes, and romantic relationships of adolescents raised by same-sex parents and a matched comparison group of adolescents raised by opposite-sex couples. No differences were reported in adolescents' psychosocial adjustment, which included depressive symptoms, anxiety, and self-esteem. Also, no difference was found for measures of school adjustment, such as academic achievement, trouble in school, or feelings of school connectedness, and no differences were found in romantic attractions or behaviors.[36]

In 2009, Abbie Goldberg analyzed one hundred studies of lesbian mothers.[37] She concluded that their children differ from those of heterosexual parents in just a few ways. Children raised by lesbian mothers tended to be less stereotypical in their gender roles and beliefs. Compared to daughters of straight parents, daughters raised by lesbians were more likely to play with toys that boys typically prefer and enjoy roughhousing. Also, about 50 percent were interested in male-typical careers, such as becoming a doctor or a lawyer, compared to only about 20 percent of daughters of heterosexual couples. The sexual preference of their parents didn't have an influence on the career aspirations of male children. About 95 percent of the sons of both lesbian and heterosexual couples were interested in male-typical careers. Compared to the children of straight couples, the children of lesbian couples do not differ in the number of friends they had, the nature of their relationship with their parents, or their overall psychological well being. However, they appear to be more tolerant of racial and ethnic differences, no doubt in part because they grew up knowing what it is like to be different.

Many of the behavioral differences stem from the fact that lesbian couples are less likely than heterosexual couples to impose gender-based expectations on their children or on themselves. They are more open to the toys their children play with, the way their children dress, and their children's career aspirations. Children of lesbian couples grow up seeing women handling and typically sharing all responsibilities and chores, while children of heterosexual couples typically see chores and responsibilities divided along gender lines, and less equally shared.

How do children raised by grandparents compare to children raised by nongrandparents?

According to the US Census Bureau, about 10 percent of all children under the age of eighteen live with at least one grandparent. Just under two-thirds of these children live in their grandparents' home.[38] Approximately 40 percent of children who live in their grandparents' homes are being cared for by their grandparent(s), and about 20 percent of grandparents raising children live below the poverty level.[39] As mentioned earlier in this chapter, poor parents face a number of challenges that aren't typically faced by parents of means, including living in neighborhoods with poorer schools and higher crime rates.

As previously discussed, even under the best conditions parenting is both challenging and stressful. Many grandparent caregivers experience additional stress, anger, and often guilt because their own child isn't there to raise their grandchildren, and because they have to deal with their grandchildren mourning the loss or absence of their parents. It may also be embarrassing for grandparents to explain the absence of their grandchildren's parents if the reason is due to incarceration, psychological problems, substance abuse, neglect, abandonment, or physical or mental abuse. Grandparents may also resent their child passing parenting responsibilities on to them, as well as the loss of their leisure time. All of this takes its toll on the physical and mental health of grandparents, which impacts their ability to raise their grandchildren. Compared to grandparents who are not responsible for raising children, those who are have been found to be more likely to experience isolation, anxiety, and depression, as well as elevated blood pressure, diabetes, heart disease, and insomnia.[40]

However, many grandparents derive considerable pleasure and fulfillment from raising their grandchildren. They enjoy the opportunity to be given a second chance at parenting and to have an important "purpose" for this part of their lives. In cases where the biological parents are capable but unavailable, such as in cases of military deployment, and grandparents volunteer to raise their grandchildren, issues of resentment and embarrassment are minimized.

Because of the likelihood of a less than ideal start in life, possibly due to poor prenatal and early postnatal care, prenatal drug/alcohol exposure, parental neglect or abuse, and parental loss (abandonment, death, and incarceration), it is difficult to evaluate how successful grandparents are at raising their grandchildren. Children who experience a difficult start in life cannot be expected to do as well as children who have a good start. However, a recent large national study found that children ages four to seventeen being raised by custodial grandmothers had more emotional symptoms, more conduct problems, more peer problems, more antisocial behavior, and more problems with inattentiveness and hyperactivity than children raised by nongrandparents.[41] However, if the grandparents had not assumed responsibility for raising their grandchildren, the outcome problems identified might have been worse.

Considering the poorer outcome data and the emotional needs of the grandchildren associated with the temporary or permanent loss of their biological parents, grandparents would likely benefit from participating in parent education programs. In addition to helping them learn how to better deal with the emotional needs of their grandchildren and hone their parenting skills, program participation would enable them to keep up-to-date with modern concerns, such as STDs, cyber-bullying, the use of recreational drugs, and the illegal misuse of prescription drugs. However, they may be reluctant to participate in parent-education programs, in part because they would be older than most other participants, and in part because participating might imply that they were inadequately prepared to do a good job when raising their own children.

WHAT SPECIAL CHALLENGES DO ADOPTIVE PARENTS FACE?

Recognizing the special challenges that adoptive parents face in meeting the mental-health and developmental needs of approximately 1.6 million adopted children, [42] the Evan B. Donaldson Adoption Institute issued the follow policy recommendation:

Parent preparation, education and support should be mandatory components of the adoption process for everyone facilitating adoptions. Furthermore, parent preparation and education should be ongoing procedures that begin during the application and homestudy phase and continue throughout the post-adoption period. For professionals who are unable to provide appropriate pre- and post-adoption services, best-practice standards require that they be knowledgeable about relevant community resources and provide appropriate referrals to their clients.[43]

At some point in time, virtually all adoptive children want to learn about their biological roots. This is a natural curiosity and usually isn't related to dissatisfaction with their adoptive family. They want to know who their biological parents are and why they were put up for adoption. They are also interested in learning about other genetically related family members, including any siblings or half-siblings. Interest often peaks during adolescence when teens are dealing with identity issues. They are trying to understand who they are and decide who they would like to become. Adoptive teens have a lot to sort though in attempting to understand who they are, since they have two sets of parents who have had an influence on them. One set they know well, and the other set they typically know little about. They may be reluctant to search for information about their biological parents or arrange a meeting with them for fear of being disloyal to their adoptive parents and offending them. It is important for adoptive parents to understand this natural curiosity and to avoid taking this personally and becoming upset. They should provide whatever information they have about the biological parents. Withholding information is a type of dishonesty, and should the child find this out, he/she will be less likely to trust the adoptive parents. Pressure should not be put on the adopted child to search for information about biological relatives, but should they be interested in doing so, help should be offered.

Part of the process of establishing identity is for teens to separate from their parents and become independent and self-directed. Some adoptive teens are reluctant to pull away from their adoptive parents because they feel that doing so would show a lack of gratitude for people who went out of their way to make a better life for a child who wasn't biologically theirs. They may also be reluctant to pull away for fear of rejection and abandonment. After all, if their biological parents abandoned them, then if they upset their adoptive parents by pulling away, perhaps they too will abandon them. If parents sense reluctance on the part of their teen to become independent, whether they are adopted or not adopted, they should do what they can to encourage the separation process. Part of chapter six, "Parenting Adolescents," deals with helping teens establish their independence. Finally, it is also important to gently warn a child who wants to meet his/her biological parents that they might not measure up to be the wonderful people the child hopes they will be.

Some adopted children wonder if their birth parents didn't want them because there was something wrong with them, especially if their adoptive parents have not shared what they know about the reason(s) the children were put up for adoption. This type of thinking can lower self-esteem. Many adopted children also grieve for their "lost" biological parents and family members. Especially around holiday time, when family members tend to gather, adoptive children may feel some degree of sadness and wonder where their biological family members are. They may also feel some degree of guilt for mourning the loss of a family they never really had when they already have a caring adoptive family.

Another concern that some adoptive children have is not looking like their adoptive parents and other family members, especially if they are of a different racial background. They may feel uncomfortable because of the questions and reactions from others, especially peers, and feel a bit out of place. At first, they may question if they really belong in the adoptive family. The amount of appearance discomfort experienced by about 17 percent of children whose adoptive parents are of a different race tends to be less when the children live in a racially diverse neighborhood.[44]

Depending upon the age of the child at the time of adoption and the previous history, attachment issues may also be a concern. As explained in chapter two, "Giving Children the Best Possible Start," warm, caring parents who enjoy interacting with their child and who are available and highly responsive to their child's needs are likely to establish a secure attachment. Many adoptive children haven't had this kind of early care, and hence have not formed a secure attachment and may have not learned to trust others. As a result, they may have trouble bonding with their adoptive parents and, later in life, forming close relationships with other people. If early-in-life adopted children have been physically or sexually abused by a caregiver, the caregiver comes to be associated with both fear and reassurance, and there is about an 80 percent chance that a type of disorganized attachment will develop. Children who develop this type of attachment are more likely to act out, be aggressive, and experience depression and anxiety. They may even have dissociative symptoms, including trancelike states (possibly as a defense against abusive caregivers). They may at times seem confused or in a fog, and they tend to be accident-prone.[45, 46]

If adopted children had a good start and securely bonded to their birth parents, but had been in the care of multiple families before being adopted, they may be reluctant to establish a close relationship with their caretakers, because each time they have done so in the past they were emotionally hurt by a separation. Also, fear of abandonment may make it difficult for adoptive children to spend time away from home. Adoptive parents need to consistently express that they care though their words and actions, and be very patient. It may take a considerable amount of time for the adoptive child to form a close emotional attachment with the adoptive parents and come to trust them and feel comfortable leaving home. Finally, because in most adoptions a probationary period precedes adoption finalization, some adoptive parents may initially be hesitant to fully bond with their adoptive child for fear that the adoption might be rescinded for reasons beyond their control, such as the birth parents changing their minds.

To various degrees, sibling rivalry occurs in all families with more than one child. In cases where some of the children are biological and some are adopted, a more intense rivalry will likely develop. When parents invest time, energy, or resources in a biological child, an adoptive child may wonder if that child is receiving favored treatment because they are the "flesh and blood" of their parents. When parents invest time, energy, or resources in an adoptive child, the biological children may think to themselves that if their parents didn't choose to adopt this child, the time, energy, or resources would have been directed their way.

Setting limits and enforcing rules may be difficult when adoptive parents feel sorry for all of the turmoil that their child may have experienced before the adoption, or are fearful that the child will not love them if they are strict. This may lead to a more permissive parenting style, which isn't in the child's best interest. When pressure is put on adoptive children to abide by rules that they don't like or when they are punished for rule violations, they may wonder if their biological parents would have been as strict. At times when they are unhappy, they may fantasize a wonderful life that could have been had they remained with their biological parents. All of this can complicate establishing and enforcing rules and policies.

Although there has been limited research done on same-sex parents who adopt, it appears that they make fine adoptive parents and are particularly effective with older children who have had multiple foster-care placements.[47] Considering all of the issues adopted children must deal with and the fact that many didn't receive the best prenatal care or the best early-life experiences, it is not surprising that they grow up with more problems than children who are not adopted. About 2 percent of American children are adopted, yet a large number of studies have determined that many times that number experience adjustment problems, especially of the more severe type that require inpatient treatment.[48, 49]

The older the child at the time of adoption, the greater the number of adjustment problems.[50] As adolescents, adoptees are more likely to use illicit drugs, engage in antisocial behavior (e.g., get into fights, destroy property), experience negative emotions (e.g., feel sad, anxious, worried, upset), do poorly in school, be less optimistic, be less self-confident, and be more disconnected from their adoptive parents. They are also about twice as likely to be diagnosed as having attention deficit hyperactivity disorder (ADHD) and oppositional defiant disorder (ODD).[51] However, adoptees have been found to engage in more pro-social behavior (e.g., help others in need) than non-adoptees.[52]

Part of the reason that adoptees are more likely to be treated for adjustment problems is that their adoptive parents tend to be older and better educated, and may be more likely to identify problems and seek out help for their children than parents who don't adopt. They also have a higher income and can better afford to pay for therapy.[53] In addition, they may seek out help more often because they found pre- and post-adoption counseling to have been helpful for them and may therefore be more pro-counseling. Finally, adoptive parents may expect more problems to develop because of their child's early-life experiences, and therefore may be more likely to see any problem that develops as not their "fault," which would make it easier to reach out for help.

While adopted children have an increased incidence of adjustment problems, the vast majority do just fine. Also, a number of studies have shown that adopted children have fewer problems than those raised in institutions or by foster parents.[54]

SUMMARY

Because of changing societal patterns, less than half of children today spend their entire childhood living with and being raised by both of their biological parents. Decades of research have shown that children raised by single parents, a single parent and a stepparent, adoptive parents, or grandparents typically have more problems than children raised by both of their biological parents.

Much of the negative impact that divorce has on children can be attributed to the manner in which the parents handled both their marriage and their divorce. Among other things, a high level of parental conflict before, during, and after a divorce takes a great toll on children. Therefore, it is extremely important that parents get along in a civil manner at all times. If the only way to accomplish this is for a divorce to take place, then for the good of the children the parents should get divorced. In addition to carefully explaining to children why a decision has been made to get divorced, the chapter discusses the things that parents can do to minimize the negative impact that divorce has on children. However, even a divorce that is handled in the best possible manner is still stressful for all family members and tends to result in children growing up very quickly.

In general, heterosexual parents and same-sex parents are quite similar in their personal characteristics, their approach to raising children, and their success as parents. However, one difference that has been frequently reported is that same-sex parents place fewer gender-related restrictions on their children, and their children are more tolerant of racial and ethnic differences. Children who are raised by their grandparents or who are adopted experience more problems than children who are raised by their parents. Because these two groups of children often don't have the best start in life, it is difficult to determine if it is their poor start or their family configuration that is responsible for the greater number of problems they typically experience.

Chapter 6
Parenting Adolescents

- Should parents look forward to the adolescent years with fear and trepidation?
- What are some general things that parents can do to reduce the chances of their adolescent children engaging in a variety of risky behaviors?
- What are some specific things that parents can do to reduce the chances of their adolescent children engaging in risky sexual behavior?
- What are some specific things that parents can do to reduce the chances of their adolescent children misusing drugs?
- How can parents minimize or even avoid the development of a parent-child power struggle during the adolescent years?
- What can parents do to help children establish their autonomy in advance of becoming adolescents?
- What can parents do to moderate the influences of peers on their adolescent children?
- How can parents help their adolescent children deal with identity issues?

Should parents look forward to the adolescent years with fear and trepidation?

There are many good reasons for parents to worry about the adolescent years. For one thing, it is during this period of time that children are intent on establishing their independence, and parents begin to realize that their influence and control is dwindling while at the same time peer influence (and sometimes control) is increasing. This is very disconcerting, because adolescents have many more opportunities than ever before to spend time with peers and to engage in risky behaviors. In fact, a recent survey found that over 50 percent of high-school students engaged in two or more risky behaviors.[1] Compared to decisions and mistakes made during childhood, those made during adolescence are much more likely to have lifelong consequences.

Having unsafe sex is one of the risky behaviors that adolescents are likely to engage in; parents worry a lot about it, and rightly so. Just over one-third of ninth-grade students and just under two-thirds of twelfth-grade students in the United States have engaged in sexual intercourse.[2] Because less than 50 percent of sexually active teens reliably use protection, the incidence of unplanned pregnancies and sexually transmitted infections (STIs) are both alarmingly high. A recent survey found that the average sexually active adolescent (ages fifteen to twenty-one) engaged in about twenty unprotected sex acts during the previous ninety day period.[3] About 14 percent of all fourteen- to fifteen-year-old females and about 24 percent of all fourteen- to nineteen-year-old females have contracted a STI.[4] Naturally, prevalence varies by number of years of sexual activity and number of lifetime partners. About 50 percent of adolescent females who have been sexually active for at least two years or who have had three or more lifetime partners have contracted a STI.

About 15 percent of sexually active females ages fifteen to nineteen become pregnant each year. About one-third of those pregnancies are terminated by abortion.[5]

Another important concern of parents of adolescents is drug use, since usage is quite common among teens and associated with a number of negative consequences. These include engaging in risky behavior (such as unplanned and unsafe sex), school failure, accidents, crime, violence, suicide, and abuse of drugs later in life, as well as many health risks, including high blood pressure, stroke, heart disease, cirrhosis of the liver, and brain damage. [6,7]

In 2005, the National Institute of Drug Abuse reported that 21.4 percent of eighth-graders, 38.2 percent of tenth-graders, and 50.4 percent of twelfth-graders had used illicit drugs at some time in their lifetime.[8] Marijuana was by far the most prevalent of the illicit drugs, which 16.5 percent of eighth-graders, 34.1 percent of tenth-graders, and 44.8 percent of twelfth-graders have used sometime in their lifetime. When it comes to using illicit drugs other than marijuana, 12.1 percent of eighth-graders, 18 percent of tenth-graders, and 27.4 percent of twelfth-graders had done so in their lifetime.

Overall, alcohol is the most problematic drug used by adolescents and young adults. The proportion of eighth-, tenth-, and twelfth-graders who reported being drunk at least once in their lifetime was 19.5 percent, 42.1 percent, and 57.5 percent, respectively.[9] In that study, binge-drinking was defined as consuming five or more drinking in a row during the prior two-week period. The proportion of eighth-, tenth-, and twelfth-graders who reported recent binge-drinking was 10.5 percent, 21.0 percent, and 27.1 percent, respectively. In a comprehensive 2007 study conducted in British Colombia, the rate of binge-drinking (in the previous thirty-day period) among young adults ages eighteen to twenty-five was reported to be 41.9 percent, and about 70 percent of British Columbia college students reported binge-drinking at some time during their lifetime.[10] Similar rates of binge-drinking have been reported for US college students.[11]

In a 2007 national Youth Risk Behavior Survey (YRBS), 29.1 percent of high-school students reported that in the thirty-day period before the survey, they had ridden at least once in a car or vehicle driven by someone who had been drinking alcohol, and 10.5 percent reported that they had driven a car or vehicle at least once when they had been drinking alcohol.[12]

According to a study in *Pediatrics*, "Use of alcohol at an early age is associated with future alcohol-related problems. Data from the National Longitudinal Alcohol Epidemiologic Study substantiated that the prevalence of both lifetime alcohol dependence and alcohol abuse show a striking decrease with increasing age at onset of use. For those aged 12 years or younger at first use, the prevalence of lifetime alcohol dependence was 40.6%, whereas those who initiated at 18 years was 16.6% and at 21 years was 10.6%. Similarly, the prevalence of lifetime alcohol abuse was 8.3% for those who initiated use at 12 years or younger, 7.8% for those who initiated at 18 years, and 4.8% for those who initiated at 21 years."[13]

Since complete maturation of the human brain doesn't occur until the late twenties, adolescent and young-adult brains are still developing. The frontal lobes, which play an important role in response inhibition, impulse control, self-insight, planning, and organization, are among the last parts of the brain to fully mature. Evidence is accumulating that alcohol consumption during adolescence can interfere with the maturation of the frontal lobes.[14] Also, consumption of large amounts of alcohol over the course of many years is associated with atrophy of parts of the brain important in memory, including the hippocampus.[15]

When it came to tobacco, a 2005 survey found that 25.9 percent of eighth-graders, 38.9 percent of tenth-graders, and 50 percent of twelfth-graders had smoked cigarettes at some time during their lifetime, but within the last thirty days only 12.1 percent of eighth-graders, 18 percent of tenth-graders, and 27.4 percent of twelfth-graders reported that they had smoked cigarettes.[16]

Adolescents who are depressed, have low self-esteem, and don't fit in are more likely to have serious drug problems, as well as those who have a family history of drug abuse.[17]

WHAT ARE SOME GENERAL THINGS THAT PARENTS CAN DO TO REDUCE THE CHANCES OF THEIR ADOLESCENT CHILDREN ENGAGING IN A VARIETY OF RISKY BEHAVIORS?

Parents need to lead by example. If they want their children to avoid engaging in risky behaviors, they need to set an example by taking good care of themselves. This means not only avoiding doing risky things like smoking, drinking irresponsibly, or speeding in a car, but they also need to actively engage in healthy behaviors like exercising regularly, eating a nutritious diet, and getting an adequate amount of sleep. When parents express through both their words and their actions the importance of staying in good health and not taking unnecessary risks, their children are much more likely to follow suit.

As discussed in chapter three, "Building Self-Esteem," there are many things that parents can do to help build their children's self-esteem, which will reduce the chances of the children succumbing to peer pressure (including boyfriend/girlfriend pressure) and engaging in risky behaviors in which they would rather not participate. Children who think highly of themselves can better afford to risk the rejection of peers because of their refusal to participate in questionable activities. To help children stand up to peer pressure, parents should also teach assertiveness skills. They can role-play with their children how to avoid being pressured into doing things they don't want to do. Finally, those high in self-esteem are less likely to become depressed, and depression in adolescence has been found to be associated with a wide variety of risk-taking behaviors.[18]

Self-directed children—who have learned how to make their own decisions and manage their own affairs—are better prepared to deal with the challenges of adolescence than children who have been parent-directed and who have not learned these skills. Adolescents typically spend large amounts of time not directly supervised by their parents or other adults. During those times, they will be faced with making a number of potentially life-altering decisions, such as whether to become sexually active or to partake in drug use. If they have not had much experience making their own decisions, they are much more likely to be impulsive and fail to consider the long-term consequences of their actions. They are also much more likely to allow others, in this case their peers, to influence their decisions. Considering the large percentage of adolescents who engage in unsafe sex and who misuse drugs, it is extremely important that by the time adolescence arrives, children are experienced and confident in their decision-making ability.

Parental expectations and attitudes can dramatically influence adolescent behavior. Without realizing it, in a variety of ways most parents convey to children that when they become adolescents they are expected to do wild and crazy things. When children are young, it isn't uncommon for them to hear parents and other adults commenting on the behavior of adolescents who live in their communities, or who are depicted on TV or in the movies. What they hear generally convinces them that risky behavior is expected of adolescents and not a big deal. In a sense, they are being given "advance permission" to behave in irresponsible ways when they get older. Another way that permission is "granted" is when they hear their parents joyfully reminiscing about the stupid things they did as teens, without mention of the serious consequences that could have resulted. It is extremely important for parents to communicate to their children that they expect them to behave in responsible ways, regardless of their age.

An authoritarian parenting style has been found to increase the chances that adolescents will engage in risky behavior.[19] As mentioned in chapter four, "Discipline and Parenting Styles," an authoritarian parenting style creates a parent-directed child who is likely to be rebellious when the parents are not around. One way that adolescents can rebel is by engaging in behaviors that their parents have prohibited. This is one way they can prove to themselves that they are no longer under their parents' control and establish the independence that is being "denied" to them by their parents.

A permissive/indulgent parenting style provides little supervision or guidance and is associated with the development of low self-esteem. Unsupervised adolescents and those with low self-esteem (especially in relationship to family and school) are more likely to engage in risk-taking behaviors. [20, 21, 22]

An authoritative parenting style provides the guidance and supervision that children and adolescents need, and at the same time encourages them to become self-directed, fosters the development of their self-esteem, and reduces their risk-taking behavior. A review of studies published between 1996-2007 on parenting style and risk-taking behaviors of adolescents found that having authoritative parents was associated with a reduced probability of engaging in behaviors that contribute to unintentional injuries and violence, tobacco use, alcohol and other drug use, unintended pregnancy and sexually transmitted diseases, and unhealthy dietary behaviors.[23]

WHAT ARE SOME SPECIFIC THINGS THAT PARENTS CAN DO TO REDUCE THE CHANCES OF THEIR ADOLESCENT CHILDREN ENGAGING IN RISKY SEXUAL BEHAVIOR?

In addition to being a good role model, building children's self-esteem, encouraging children to be self-directed, conveying positive expectations, and using an authoritative parenting style, there are some specific things that parents can do to reduce the chances of their adolescent children engaging in risky sexual behavior.

Unfortunately, many parents don't discuss safe sex in advance of their teens becoming sexually active. A recent study found that about 60 percent of boys and girls ages thirteen to seventeen reported that they engaged in sexual intercourse before their parents talked about how to use a condom.[24] Also, about 55 percent of boys and about 40 percent of girls had intercourse before their parents spoke with them about birth control. Finally, about 40 percent of both boys and girls reported that they had had sexual intercourse before their parents talked with them about what to do if their partner refused to use a condom.

In order to avoid the uncomfortable feeling that both parents and children often experience when having the "big talk" about sex, parents should start with small discussions when their children are very young. The goal is for parents to have an informative ongoing dialogue with their children about sex. Children should be provided with age-appropriate information, and parents should answer all of their questions but not elaborate with more details than their children are ready to hear. A good starting point is to help children learn the names and locations of body parts, including genitals. A discussion of "good touch" and "bad touch" should be included. Pregnant family members or friends can serve as a springboard for discussions about sexual maturation, sexual intercourse, and conception. Mother-adolescent discussions about condom use *before* first sexual intercourse has been shown to dramatically increase condom use during first intercourse and thereafter.[25]

TV programs that contain sexual content can also serve as a stimulus for discussing a wide variety of sexual topics. All types of sexual activity, including masturbation and homosexual relationships, should be discussed. Abstinence, responsibility, consequences, and values should be part of the dialogue. Since the likelihood of practicing safe sex is related to perceptions of the probability of pregnancy and contracting an STI, parents should make sure that *in advance of their children becoming sexually active* they understand the high risks associated with unsafe sex.[26] Parents should discuss the pleasurable aspects of intimacy and sexual activity as well.

Some teens who do not feel special or well cared for may seek out a sexual relationship to help meet those needs. The kinds of things that they are typically told by their sexual partner(s) help them to feel good about themselves. They may also want to have a child to ensure that someone is there who will always love them. In order to avoid this deficit-need-filling motivation, parents should be sure to tell their children that they are loved and provide unconditional positive regard as discussed in chapter three, "Building Self-Esteem." In cases where there is an absent father, adolescent females may use sex as a way to gain male attention. Single mothers who involve male figures, such as uncles, in their daughters' lives can reduce the chances of this happening.

Children who engage in family activities, who feel close to their parents, and whose parents have knowledge of their friends and activities—as is typically the case where an authoritative parenting style has been used—are less likely to engage in risky sexual behaviors.[27]

About 23 percent of teen pregnancies are intentional.[28] Some of these teens are married and want to start a family, others are not. Teens who intentionally become pregnant typically do not have future plans that having a child would interfere with. They see becoming a parent as something of value that they can accomplish, usually without considering all that is required to care for a child. There are many things that parents can do to help their children acquire a healthy level of achievement motivation so that they will strive to accomplish valuable things in addition to having children. A thorough discussion of this takes place in chapter seven, "Fostering Achievement." Finally, female teenagers may be motivated to become pregnant in order to get positive attention from family members and friends, since being a pregnant teen is now often viewed as a status symbol rather than as a shameful situation.

When parents treat adolescents as if they were young children, the adolescents develop a need to prove to themselves that they are mature. One way to accomplish that is to engage in adult behaviors, such as becoming sexually active and drinking alcohol. When parents treat their adolescents in an adult-like manner, the teens' need to prove to themselves that they are "all grown up" is reduced.

WHAT ARE SOME SPECIFIC THINGS THAT PARENTS CAN DO TO REDUCE THE CHANCES OF THEIR ADOLESCENT CHILDREN MISUSING DRUGS?

In addition to being a good role model, building children's self-esteem, encouraging children to become self-directed, conveying positive expectations, and using an authoritative parenting style, there are some specific things that parents can do to reduce the chances of their adolescent children misusing drugs.

By far, the drug that causes the most problems for adolescents is alcohol. This of course is a drug that is readily available and one that adolescents often see their parents and other adults openly using, especially at parties and celebrations. While about two-thirds of twelfth graders don't approve of binge-drinking (defined in this study as having five or more drinks once or twice each weekend), only 45 percent viewed binge-drinking on weekends as carrying a great risk.[29] Young adults have even more favorable attitudes toward drinking. During over forty years as a college professor, I have often discussed binge-drinking with my students. One of the most disconcerting things I have learned through those discussions is that most do not view binge-drinking as a problem or something that they would like to eliminate or even reduce. In fact, many see excessive drinking as something that is both socially acceptable and highly desirable. Relatively few students are concerned about the consequences of binge-drinking, even though about 2,100 alcohol-related traffic accidents occur each year among sixteen- to twenty-year-olds, and over 4,500 alcohol-related deaths occur annually among sixteen to twenty-four-year-olds.[30, 31] This accepting attitude toward binge-drinking no doubt results in part from what child development expert David Elkind called the personal fable, a form of egocentrism (self-centeredness) commonly exhibited by adolescents.[32] Many adolescents and young adults see negative consequences of alcohol consumption as something that may happen to other people but not to them. They see themselves as special and possessing an exaggerated sense of invulnerability. Unless attitudes can be changed, it is unlikely that binge-drinking will decline. Parents, of course, are partially responsible for the attitudes that their children develop. It is crucial for parents to convey the importance of responsible drinking through both their words and actions.

It is also important for parents to be sure that their children understand the behavioral and health risks associated with heavy drinking. As children age, peer influence increases and parental influence decreases, but parents can still play an important role, especially if children have a close relationship with them. College freshmen have been found to be less likely to binge-drink if their parents talked with them about binge-drinking shortly before they started college.[33] In addition, encouraging children to seek out both friends and social activities that aren't alcohol-focused would definitely be helpful.[34] Parental supervision and monitoring during adolescence, which includes knowing where children are and what they are doing, have been strongly linked with whether adolescents develop friendships with drug-using peers and, in turn, become drug users.[35] Those who are less closely supervised are more likely to form friendships with drug users.

Finally, parents need to be able to spot the warning signs of teenage alcohol and drug use so that they can identify problems early and get their children the help they need. The American Academy of Child and Adolescent Psychiatry has identified the following signs of alcohol and drug use:[36]

- **Physical**—fatigue, repeated health complaints, red and glazed eyes, lasting cough
- **Emotional**—personality change, sudden mood changes, irritability, low self-esteem, irresponsible behavior, poor judgment, depression, a general lack of interest
- **Family**—starting arguments, breaking rules, withdrawing from the family
- **School**—decreased interest, negative attitude, drop in grades, many absences, truancy, discipline problems
- **Social problems**—new friends who are less interested in standard home and school activities, problems with the law, changes to less-conventional styles in dress and music

HOW CAN PARENTS MINIMIZE OR EVEN AVOID THE DEVELOPMENT OF A PARENT-CHILD POWER STRUGGLE DURING THE ADOLESCENT YEARS?

Adolescence is a transition period between childhood and adulthood. Most adolescents want to run their own lives just like adults do, while most parents do not feel that they are ready to do so. As parents begin to realize that their children are growing up and spending more time away from them and unsupervised, they typically begin to worry that the children will get into trouble. Worried parents, including those who have generally practiced an authoritative parenting style, often start to place restrictions on their adolescent children, hoping to reduce the chances of the children getting into trouble. So at a time when the adolescents want their freedom, parents often become more controlling. This may create a power struggle—one that need not occur.[37]

If the parenting style in use is authoritarian, the struggle will likely be more intense, since an underlying goal of authoritarian parents is to raise parent-directed children. In cases where authoritarian parents use very harsh punishment, in the presence of the parents the children may comply, and it will appear to the parents that a power struggle is not underway. However, the typically rebellious behavior of unsupervised adolescents raised by strict parents tells a very different story. Also, the more controlling parents are, the more likely adolescents will seek guidance from peers.[38] If the parents practice a permissive parenting style, where just about anything goes, a power struggle will not occur, but other serious problems will, such as low self-esteem and low achievement motivation.

The way to minimize and possibly prevent the development of a parent-adolescent power struggle is for parents to help their children to become self-directed in advance of becoming adolescents. As discussed in chapter four, "Discipline and Parenting Styles," children are most likely to become self-directed when raised using an authoritative parenting style. Parents who raise self-directed children are more likely to have confidence in the children's ability to manage their own lives, and hence the parents will be less worried and feel less of a need to place restrictions on the children when they become adolescents. In a sense then, by helping children to establish autonomy in advance of adolescence, parents can avoid or at least minimize the power-struggle issues, and children will be better prepared to deal with the challenges that adolescence presents.

During arguments with parents, adolescents often get emotional and say things that parents find offensive. This in part is due to the dramatic hormonal changes that occur in early adolescence. Parents tend to take these offensive statements very personally. They often feel hurt and rejected and may overreact, intensifying the conflict that underlies the argument. It is best for parents to try to remain calm and resist yelling or punishing the child for making offensive statements. However, by expressing how these statements make them feel, parents are able to help their adolescent children learn about how their behavior impacts others. For example, if during a heated argument an adolescent were to say, "I hate you—you are the worst dad in the entire world," a parent might immediately want to lash back at the child and make a "you" type of statement that attacks the child, perhaps saying something like, "I wish I weren't your father—you are just an unappreciative brat." Instead, the father should try to remain calm and communicate how the child's statement makes him feel by making an "I" type of statement, perhaps saying something like, "When I hear you say that, I feel very sad and a bit angry, since there is nothing more important to me than being a good father, and I believe that I have worked hard at doing so." Communicating how the offensive statement makes the parent feel helps the adolescent to develop empathy, an essential quality of a caring person.

When parents make it clear that they trust and respect their adolescent children, their children are much less likely to feel a need to challenge their parents or to engage in rebellious behavior. They understand that if they do "stupid" things, they risk losing that trust and respect. On the other hand, adolescents who don't feel trusted or respected by their parents have a lot less to lose by challenging their parents and entering power struggles or by engaging in rebellious behavior, and hence are more likely to do so.

One way that parents can convey that they trust and respect their adolescent children is to give them the responsibility of taking care of younger siblings. It is important that this be done in a way that is not viewed by the adolescent as burdensome. One way to accomplish this is to *ask* the adolescent if he/she is willing to take care of a younger sibling, rather than to *require* it. Another way to accomplish this is to offer to pay the adolescent the amount of money that a babysitter would normally get for providing this service. Initially, the period of care should be short to ensure that the siblings get along with each other. Another option that encourages cooperation on the part of a younger sibling is for the older sibling to offer to share part of what he/she is earning from babysitting with the younger sibling, providing that they are cooperative.

WHAT CAN PARENTS DO TO HELP CHILDREN ESTABLISH THEIR AUTONOMY IN ADVANCE OF BECOMING ADOLESCENTS?

Parents need to start very early if they want to raise children who have most of the skills needed to effectively manage their lives by the time they reach adolescence. Essentially, parents need to teach children not to need them. One of the most effective ways to accomplish this is for parents to adopt a "guide and step aside" philosophy. This philosophy is consistent with the authoritative style of parenting but stresses letting children make their own decisions and experience doing things for themselves. The section of chapter three, "Building Self-Esteem," that focuses on "Expressing Confidence in the Child" contains some specific examples of how to start this process, so that children grow to become both functionally and emotionally independent. One of the strategies introduced in that section that will be more thoroughly developed here is giving a child an allowance.

Almost all parents provide children with money to buy things. By giving children an allowance, parents are helping them learn how to make decisions about spending "their" money. Parents who don't give a child an allowance place themselves in the decision-making role. Based on their children's requests, they decide what the children will and will not be allowed to buy. An experience I had nicely illustrates this. My wife and I began giving our first child, Karen, an allowance when she was five years old. About two months later, we went to an annual local charity fund-raising event called "Hot Dog Day" that is put on by students attending the two institutions of higher education that are located in our small village in Alfred, New York. The event is much like a street fair.

As we were leaving our house to go to Hot Dog Day, we had to get around a bunch of balloons near the doorway that Karen had brought home from a birthday party she had attended the previous day. As we arrived at Hot Dog Day, Karen said to me, "Dad, will you buy me a Hot Dog Day balloon?" I wasn't surprised by this request, since many of the children we saw there were holding balloons, and in previous years I had always bought her one. However, since we already had a bunch of balloons floating around at home, I was a bit reluctant to purchase yet another one. So I said, "Karen, if you really want a balloon, you can use some of your allowance money to buy one." In response, she said, "I think I'll look around first, Dad, and see what else there is to buy before deciding if I want to spend some of my allowance on a balloon." Had she not had an allowance, I would have been the one deciding on whether to purchase the balloon, but since she had an allowance she was now put in the decision-making position. By the way, that day she spent her money on more interesting things and never did buy a Hot Dog Day balloon, which was just fine with me.

If you believe as I do that an allowance is a good tool to help children establish their autonomy, then there are a number of allowance-related things to be considered, such as at what age will the allowance begin, how often will the allowance be given, what will be the starting amount, will the amount change as the child gets older, will completing chores be tied to receiving the allowance, just how much parental guidance will be provided regarding the spending of the money, and at what age will the allowance be stopped.

Starting Age: Since most children do not have the mathematical ability to understand money and how much change adds up to a dollar until they are five to seven years old, starting an allowance sooner than that isn't advisable. Some would argue that even if children can do the math, it is best to wait until they are older, since starting an allowance at an early age places a lot of emphasis on money, and our society is already too materialistic.

Frequency: With younger children, it is best to provide a weekly allowance. With older children, it might make sense to provide an allowance on a biweekly or monthly basis. Extending the amount of time helps older children learn how to delay gratification and to plan/budget.

Starting Amount: Before deciding on an amount, parents need to consider several things, including their financial circumstances, the cost of living in the area where they reside, the amount of spending money that their children's peers are likely to have, and what they would like their children to use their allowance for. Assuming that providing an allowance will not be a financial hardship for the parents, once the other things are considered an amount can be determined.

In determining a starting amount, the most important thing to consider is just what parents would like to encourage the allowance money to be used for (it should of course be the children's decision as to how to actually spend their allowance). There are four major categories for which allowances are typically used: buying items for self (toys, food, movie tickets, etc.), buying items for others (presents for family members and friends, etc.), saving for the future (to make a special purchase, go on a school trip, etc), and charity donations. This last category is not one that is often thought about, but encouraging children to give to charities, as well as role-modeling that behavior, communicates the importance of being a caring and generous person.

Amount of Guidance: Parents who adopt the philosophy of "guide and step aside" should talk with the children from time to time about how they are spending their allowance money—but avoid badgering them. Remember, children will learn about how to spend their money from both the wise and unwise choices they make. About the time that Karen was eight, we took a vacation trip by car from our home in the western part of New York state to Maine. About two hours into the trip, we stopped at a mall in Binghamton, New York. In the mall, Karen fell in love with a polar-bear stuffed animal, which was quite expensive (as I recall, about $40 back in 1989). She immediately wanted to buy it. Providing a little guidance, I reminded her of two things: there might be more interesting things to buy on this long vacation trip, and we already had fifty-two stuffed toys at home. (Just before the trip we had gathered all of the stuffed animals together that she and her sister had been given over the years—mostly not by their parents I would like to add—and placed them in a hammock hung in the corner of her bedroom, where they still sit to this very day). Being a reasonable child, she said she would wait and buy the bear on the way back home from Maine unless she found some other preferred use of her money.

As it happened, she didn't spend much money in Maine, but she hadn't mentioned the bear again since the day we left the mall. On the way back home, as we approached the mall, I remembered the bear. Not particularly wanting us to acquire a fifty-third stuffed animal, I debated with myself as to whether I should remind her that she had planned to buy it if she didn't find something else on the trip that she preferred. Because I'm a firm believer in providing guidance but letting children make their own decisions, I didn't debate very long. By the time I had said, "Karen, do you remember on the way to Maine we had stopped at a mall ..." she immediate yelled out, "The polar bear!" To my chagrin, she bought the bear, which I thought would gather dust like most of the other stuffed animals. But was I ever wrong. She named the bear "Snowflake" and took it just about every place she went for a couple of years. It actually was a good purchase that she thoroughly enjoyed.

Amount Over Time: Since children's needs and desires increase as they get older, most parents gradually increase allowance amounts, often on each birthday. Some parents believe that when children are very young, they should use their money solely for the purpose of buying things for themselves, and the parents don't encourage other categories of spending, such as buying things for others. Hence they provide a small allowance. As their children get older, they expect them to be using their allowance for other things as well, such as buying gifts for others, and increase their allowance accordingly.

As children approach adolescence, one way that parents can turn over additional control is to provide them with an allowance that is sufficiently large to cover virtually all of their expenses. Doing so is a vote of confidence in them and helps to minimize the power struggle that typically develops between adolescents who want to run their own lives and parents who still want to maintain control.

In 1993, when Karen was twelve years old, my wife and I gave her the option of becoming "financially independent" by providing her with an allowance large enough to cover all of her expenses, with the exception of food eaten with the family, medical expenses, and family trips and outings. She said that she wasn't ready to take on that amount of responsibility, so we continued the then-current allowance arrangement. The following year we made the same offer, and she accepted it on a one-year trial basis.

In order to determine what would be an adequate amount of money, I asked her to first write down everything she did that cost money, including the purchase of clothing, taking piano lessons, buying an annual ski pass, and so on. She diligently made a list of everything she could think of. I added a few things to the list, and then together we estimated the amount of money that each item cost. This was definitely an eye-opening experience for her. She was shocked when we came up with an amount of $220 per month. She had no idea that her parents were routinely spending that much money on her. Recognizing that we probably left out a few expenses, my wife and I decided to give her $250 per month, which she initially thought was an outrageously large amount. While this amount of money may appear to be very generous, especially back in 1993, it really wasn't. As indicated in chapter one,

"Getting Ready to Become a Parent," the USDA has determined that depending on income level, it currently takes an average of between $726 and $1,464 per month to cover all of the costs of raising one child to age seventeen. That of courses included expenses that are not covered by an allowance.

Andrea, the younger sister by about four years, was quite jealous and immediately said, "That's a huge amount of money; I can't wait until I'm old enough to have the same arrangement." To my great surprise, about three months later Andrea spoke with me in private and said that Karen was struggling to cover all of her expenses, and that I needed to raise her allowance. I approached Karen and offered to raise her allowance, but she said a deal was a deal and she would continue with the amount we had agreed on for the rest of the year. She liked having the independence to make her own purchase decisions; the following year she accepted an allowance increase, and we made the arrangement permanent.

This arrangement was largely successful because from a very young age Karen had been raised with a "guide and step aside" philosophy, and thus had a lot of practice making decisions years in advance of being given a relatively large amount of money to manage. Without that kind of background, it would not be advisable to give an adolescent a large amount of money and the responsibility that goes with it.

Chores and Allowance: The vast majority of parents tie allowance to the completion of chores. They do so because they believe that it is important that children learn to work for what they get. After all, that is the way that the real world operates. A small number of parents separate chores and allowance. They take the position that family resources and chores should be shared but not linked. They want their children to take responsibility for helping out because it is the right thing to do, not because there is a direct payoff for doing so. As explained in chapter four, "Discipline and Parenting Styles," when people are paid for doing things, intrinsic motivation decreases. By not paying children to do chores, any intrinsic motivation to accomplish them will be preserved. Also, when children are expected to share in chores because it is the right thing to do, they are indirectly learning to care about others and not take advantage of them.

When Should an Allowance be Stopped?: Some parents believe that a good way to teach children responsibility is to encourage them to find a job. They also believe that children's self-esteem will increase once they find someone outside of their home willing to pay them for what they are able to contribute. Finding a job may also be important, or even essential, if the family has limited resources. Since virtually all children want to have money to spend, taking away their allowances once they are old enough to work is one way to motivate them to find employment. Other parents encourage children to find employment but continue their allowances until they do so, or until they reach a certain age.

A smaller number of parents encourage children to find employment but have no plans to discontinue their allowances if they do so while they are still in school. Those parents feel that taking away an allowance is a form of negative punishment and see no reason to punish the children if they take the initiative to find work. Finally, a very small number of parents are not particularly interested in their children finding a job as long as they are making good use of their time by doing such things as studying, participating on teams or in after-school activities, or doing volunteer work. In fact, a good number of this latter group of parents would actually prefer that their children not work. They believe that the benefits gained from doing other things outweigh the benefits gained from working, and also note their children will have roughly forty years of work ahead of them to gain work related benefits. This very small group of parents tends to provide sizeable allowances as a way to reduce their children's motivation to get a job.

A recent report by the Bureau of Labor Statistics found that on average, for each hour of work outside of the home, teenagers will spend five minutes less on homework, ten minutes less on sleep, eleven minutes less on household work, and twenty-four minutes less on screen (TV and computer) time.[39] About 75 percent of high-school seniors work outside the home sometime during the school year. Working just a few hours per week doesn't appear to have a negative impact on the academic performance of high-school students, but when the number of hours worked per week gets above fifteen, grades typically suffer.[40] What often happens is that once children begin to work and earn money, they often want to work more in order to earn more and are willing to give up other activities, including important ones like studying, in order to do so. This is especially true if they do not receive any allowance, or receive a small one. A recent study found that college students' grades suffered when they worked more than twenty hours per week.[41]

WHAT CAN PARENTS DO TO MODERATE THE INFLUENCES OF PEERS ON THEIR ADOLESCENT CHILDREN?

When parents adopt an authoritative parenting style, their children typically feel respected and supported, and in turn are more likely to respect their parents and feel close to them. They will likely not want to let them down and will be less likely to rebel by doing things that would earn their parents' disapproval. This means that when these children are encouraged by peers to engage in questionable behaviors, their parents' views have a better chance of influencing the outcome.

By helping their children develop a high level of self-esteem and a good set of values, parents greatly increase the chances that the children will select desirable friends. This of course means that they will experience a more positive type of peer pressure than children who select undesirable friends. However, there are no guarantees when it comes to parenting, and sometimes adolescents select undesirable friends even when they themselves have a high level of self-esteem and a good set of values. Therefore, it is important for parents to know their children's friends. This can be accomplished in a number of ways, including having their friends spend time in the family home, perhaps by arranging parties or barbeques, or inviting friends to accompany the family on outings or trips.

If parents are concerned about the type of friends that their children are acquiring, they should try to avoid the tendency to focus on the friends' flaws and ignore positive attributes. Doing so will upset the children and likely place them in the position of wanting to defend their friends, even if on some level they recognize some of the friends' flaws.

A better approach is for parents to simply ask children to talk about each of their friends. In the course of the conversation, the parents can ask if there are any characteristics of their friends that their children particularly admire or are concerned about. Often the very concerns that the parents have are shared by their children. By using this approach, the children may become the ones who are criticizing their friends instead of their parents doing the criticizing. If the parents learn that the children share their concerns, they will be relieved and feel much less pressure to highlight the undesirable characteristics of the friends. If the children don't share the same concerns, the parents need to guide and then step aside. One way to accomplish this without putting the children too much on the defensive is to spend time first reflecting on the positive characteristics of the friends before mentioning the negative ones. Also, once the parents are sure that their children understand their concerns, they need to back off, unless they are convinced that their children's health or safety is in danger. Prohibiting children from spending time with certain friends usually doesn't work. The children find a way to sneak face-to-face time with them, and often can easily arrange to spend "cyber-time" with them.

How can parents help their adolescent children deal with identity issues?

Adolescents typically become focused on figuring out who they are and deciding on where they are headed and who they would like to become. According to Eric Erikson, who formulated the well known eight stage psychosocial theory of development, the goal of adolescents is achieving a coherent identity and avoiding identity confusion.[42] Identity is a multifaceted concept and includes an understanding of such things as one's gender, physical self and sexuality, heritage, personality, beliefs, values and goals. It is not easy to figure all of this out, and many adolescents struggle in an attempt to do so, especially if their parents have set ideas about who they are and who they should become. For example, most parents assume that their children are heterosexual and will practice the same religion (or lack thereof) that they practice. When adolescents deviate from these expectations, it can be extremely stressful if parents and other family members are critical or rejecting. Hence, many adolescents don't share their real identities with all family members and instead lead a double life, which is both difficult and stressful.

The process of achieving a coherent identity involves exploration of options (roles, values, goals) followed by commitment. Some adolescents latch onto an identity without taking the time to seriously explore options. They often commit to an identity foisted upon them by others, such as parents or cliques, or they may come to idolize a celebrity and try to be like him/her, in the process temporarily losing hold of who they really are. This is referred to as *identity foreclosure*. Later in life, they may decide that who they have become isn't who they really are deep down or who they would like to be. They may experience what is sometimes referred to as a *midlife crisis* and take on a new identity. In order to help adolescents avoid identity foreclosure, parents should try to remain open-minded and encourage exploration. This typically happens with parents who have adopted an authoritative parenting style. Parents also should realize that during the identity-search process, it isn't unusual for adolescents to have, at least temporarily, some unrealistic goals. It is best for parents to not be hypercritical and tell their adolescents to set more realistic goals. Given time, the adolescents will typically come to that conclusion themselves.

Some adolescents experience *identity moratorium*, where they have explored options but are unready to make commitments. Unfortunately, parents often view such a lack of direction as aimless wandering and a waste of time. They in turn put pressure on their children to decide on a direction. This may result in a movement from identity moratorium to identity foreclosure. It is best for parents to allow children who are experiencing identity moratorium time to figure things out. Doing so will likely increase their happiness and future success.

Upon graduation from college with a major in psychology, my younger daughter, Andrea, accepted what appeared to be an excellent position with a very large and well-known major US corporation. She had always been a high achiever and thought that such a position would allow her to continue on that path. However, she quickly learned that the nature of the work, which among other things involved very little contact with people, was not a good match for her interests and skills. After a couple of months, she quit her job. She now was in an identity moratorium state with regard to a career, because she was reluctant to commit to anything else for fear that she might not like it as well. This was a painful state for her to be in, since for the first time in her life she had both quit something and didn't have goals that she was pursuing. Over the next few years, she worked in a number of positions that she knew would not be long-term, and she spent a lot of time thinking about and researching various career options before deciding to pursue a master's degree in education, with the goal of becoming an elementary school teacher. During that period of time, my wife and I provided a bit of guidance but intentionally avoided steering her in any direction. We knew that was something she would need to figure out for herself.

Finally, some adolescents aren't interested in exploring options or in making commitments. They are not in a hurry to grow up and are in state known as *identity diffusion*. For obvious reasons, parents are troubled by this. In cases where identity diffusion continues into adulthood, some professional counseling might be helpful.

SUMMARY

Because of the high likelihood of teens engaging in risky behaviors, parents of adolescents have much to worry about. Some things that parents can do to reduce all types of risky behavior include developing a close relationship with their children by using an authoritative parenting style, being good role models, building their children's self-esteem, encouraging their children to become self-directed, and conveying positive expectations about their children's behavior. In addition, it is helpful for parents to know their children's friends and keep track of their children's whereabouts.

Typically, a power struggle develops when adolescents want to run their own lives and parents don't think that they are ready to do so. This can be minimized or even avoided if parents are able to help their children establish a good part of their autonomy in advance of becoming adolescents. It also helps if parents can remain calm when in fits of emotion their children say hurtful things to them. Finally, adolescents need to be given time to figure out who they are and what they want to do with their lives.

Chapter 7
Fostering Achievement

- How should achievement be measured?
- How can parents help children reach their full potential and become high achievers?
    a. Initial preparation for parenting
    b. Prenatal and early postnatal care
    c. Fostering attachment
    d. Self-esteem development
    e. Discipline and parenting style
    f. Role modeling
    g. Reducing inter-parental conflict
    h. Preparing for the adolescent years
- How are education and achievement related?
- How does parent involvement in children's education influence academic performance?
- Why should parents avoid pressuring children to be high achievers, especially early on?
- Why is it important for parents to provide positive regard, regardless of the level of their children's accomplishments?

How should achievement be measured?

In the extremely competitive world we live in, most parents feel that in order for the children to be happy, they will need to become high achievers. Amy Chua's recent bestselling book, the *Battle Hymn of the Tiger Mother,* illustrates this point. Parents rarely consider the possibility that children could be happy without acquiring a long list of accomplishments. In fact, by pressuring children to continuously achieve, parents typically create a self-fulfilling prophecy, because their children become convinced that excelling is the only thing that is worthwhile and the only way to please their parents. This means that children will eventually come to judge themselves more based on the performance of others than on their own effort and performance. Regardless of how hard they work or how well they perform, they will likely not be happy unless they do better than most other children. For example, a child who completes in a race and turns in a personal-best time will not consider that much of an achievement unless that time was better than the times of most or all of the other competitors. This isn't a healthy situation, because no matter how well one does, there will likely always be others who are able to perform even better. As discussed in chapter three, "Building Self-Esteem," this creates a situation in which children are destined to have low self-esteem, because almost all will come to believe that they haven't accomplished enough, since only a few can truly be top achievers.

A healthier way to measure achievement would be to compare a child's performance with his/her own potential, instead of with the performance of other children. For example, assuming a child puts serious effort into training for a race, if a personal best time was achieved, that should be considered a major accomplishment regardless of whether the child came in first, last, or somewhere in between. Because of the way most people have been raised there is resistance to looking at achievement in this way. However, with additional contemplation, the idea is often embraced.

How can parents help children reach their full potential and become high achievers?

Below is a summary of things that parents can do to foster achievement, many of which have been more fully dealt with in the preceding chapters of this book.

Initial preparation for parenting
People who prepare in advance of having children tend to be better

and happier parents. Obviously, more effective and more content parents will be better able to help their children acquire the skills and characteristics that will enable the children to become high achievers. Preparation ideally includes finding someone to coparent with who has similar views on parenting and children, learning about parenting techniques and normal child development, giving serious thought to the kind of parent you would like to become and the kind of qualities/characteristics you would like your children to develop, realizing the awesome responsibility that parenting entails and the sacrifices that will need to be made, and developing a plan to provide the time and financial resources needed.

Prenatal and early postnatal care

The focus of chapter two, "Giving Children the Best Possible Start," is helping children to reach their full neurological potential (that is, building the best possible brain). Good prenatal and early postnatal care—which includes proper nutrition and avoiding exposure to harmful substances, as well as providing early stimulation—are of fundamental importance to brain development. This includes providing an enriched home environment, and for children being cared for by others, carefully selecting a placement that not only meets their health and safety needs but their intellectual and emotional needs as well. Children who have reached their full neurological potential are best positioned to become high achievers.

Fostering attachment

Children tend to form a secure type of attachment if they have parents who are sensitive and responsive. Because securely attached children are more comfortable exploring their environment, they are likely to be exposed to more stimulation than children who have not formed a secure bond with their parents. Later in life, securely attached children often have high self-esteem and perform better in school than children who have not formed a secure attachment with their parents.

Self-esteem development

Children who have high self-esteem are confident, enjoy being challenged, and function well independently, three things that are associated with high achievement. Chapter three, "Building Self-Esteem," discusses the importance of early attachment and then focuses on six techniques for helping children develop a high, but realistic, level of self-esteem. They are:

1. Provide a safe and secure environment.
2. Always be respectful of children.
3. Use descriptive feedback.
4. Be a positive role model.
5. Express confidence in children.
6. Challenge any incorrect negative self-statements that children make.

Discipline and parenting style

Parents who view discipline as a process that focuses on teaching values and right from wrong, rather than a process that creates fear, and who use an authoritative parenting style, are likely to raise children who are self-directed and feel respected. Self-directed people are less influenced by pressure from others and are better able to follow their own passions and steer their own paths. This increases the chances that they will become high achievers.[1]

Children who have been raised using an authoritative parenting style are also more likely to become caring people. Most high-achieving people eventually are put in charge of other people. Caring supervisors often are able to gain the respect, support, and cooperation of those who they supervise. This of course increases the likelihood that those supervisors do well, get promoted, and go on to even greater accomplishments.

Role modeling

When children observe their parents working hard to accomplish goals, they are likely to want to do the same. Therefore, it is important for parents to talk with their children about their own goals and their plans for accomplishing them. This might mean explaining how they are training to run a race, saving to buy a house, or striving to get a promotion. When parents keep silent about their goals and plans, children are less likely to be motivated to achieve. Children need to know that reaching some goals takes a great deal of time. Therefore, it is also important for parents to model perseverance. They might explain that preparing for a race can take months, saving for a house can take years, and rising to the top of a company can take decades. Knowing how to get back up and try again after a failure is a component of perseverance and an important lesson for parents to teach and model.

Parents need to carefully evaluate just what role they are modeling for their children. They need to be sure that the way they spend their time reflects what they truly value. If parents say that family is most important but spend most of their time working to advance their career, they are sending a mixed message to their children. It is likely that their children will come to believe that achievement is really more important than family. Similarly, if a parent becomes depressed after being passed over for a promotion, the message being communicated is that achievement is of tremendous importance. Parental behavior of this type may result in children who become driven to achieve (overachievers). If, on the other hand, a parent is able to get back on his/her feet quickly after being passed over for a promotion, the children will learn that not succeeding doesn't have to be traumatic.

Reducing inter-parental conflict

Children who report high levels of inter-parental conflict suffer academically.[2] It is highly stressful for children to witness their parents openly fighting. Just like children often feel responsible when their parents divorce, children who experience high levels of parental conflict are likely to blame themselves for causing the conflict, which only adds to their stress level.[3] It is likely that their ability to focus on their academic work will suffer because they will be constantly thinking about family troubles. It is also likely that their parents are less available to help with schoolwork. As a result, these children often perform at a level below their potential. However, when children have a close and supportive relationship with at least one parent, and that parent closely monitors academic progress, inter-parental conflict has been found to have a reduced impact on academic performance.[4, 5]

Preparing for the adolescent years

Because of the importance of identity achievement, the potential to get off track by engaging in risky behaviors that can result in life-altering consequences, and the development of serious parent-child power struggles, the adolescent years are of crucial importance to future achievement. Significant turmoil during this period of time can stop a child who previously was a high achiever dead in his/her tracks. As discussed in the previous chapter, one strategy to reduce the chances of this happening is to help children become as independently functioning as possible before adolescence by adopting a "guide and step aside" parenting strategy early on. This strategy helps children learn how to make decisions and manage their own lives, which helps with their identity achievement and reduces the chances that they will engage in risky behaviors or enter power struggles with their parents.

HOW ARE EDUCATION AND ACHIEVEMENT RELATED?

Getting a good education is an achievement in itself, and it is also associated with financial success. According to the US Census Bureau[6], in 2007 the median annual earnings for full-time workers age twenty-five and over by educational attainment were as follows:

- Not a High-School Graduate $24,964
- High-School Graduate $32,862
- Some College or Associate's Degree $40,769
- Bachelor's Degree $56,118
- Advanced Degree $75,140

In addition to earning more money, well-educated people are more likely to succeed in other areas. They tend to be in better health, less likely to be in trouble with the law or to experience unemployment, and more likely to be involved in their communities.[7] They also tend to do well as parents. Compared to less-educated parents, they spend more time reading to their children, and their children have better concentration skills and perform better cognitively.[8]

Most children start life with a great interest in learning, in part because the more they learn, the better they are able to understand how the world works. Parents are in the ideal position to turn this interest in learning into a love of learning, and eventually a passion for education. Unfortunately, relatively few are able to accomplish this, and as children get older they typically become less interested in education. If it weren't for the financial benefits of an education, many would drop out of school as soon as they were old enough to do so.

In addition to helping build a better brain, stimulating environments also prevent boredom and help children to become curious and interested in learning. As discussed in chapter two, "Giving Children the Best Possible Start," parents should provide a wide array of interesting types of stimulation and let children select what interests them at the time. Stimulation for young children could include playing music, singing songs, drawing pictures, dancing, reading books, telling stories, building with blocks, making puzzles, learning letters and numbers, plus a host of other things. Young children often will become fixated on one type of activity for a period of time before moving on to another. Whatever that might be, parents should provide an ever-increasing complexity of stimulation. For example, once a child masters completing simple puzzles, slightly more challenging ones should be made available.

Since parents are role models, children are likely to become excited about the types of activities that their parents are interested in. If parents have a strong interest in sports and spend lots of time watching sporting events in person and/or on TV, their children are likely to do the same. If parents get excited about learning and spend lots of time seeking out new information or watching informative shows on TV, children are likely to follow suit. One of the reasons children's interest in learning fades over time is the lack of parental interest and support.

When my children were in high school, they participated in many extracurricular activities, including sports, drama, and Academic All Stars (academic team competition). I noticed that at sporting events and theatre productions, virtually every participant had a number of family members present. Also, many in attendance were community members who didn't have children who were participating. Unfortunately, that was not the case at Academic All Star competitions. At those events, often less than half of the participants had any family members in attendance, and rarely did anyone bother to come who didn't have children competing. This sends a strong message to children that being a good learner isn't nearly as important as being a good athlete or actor. Similarly, parents' failure to take an interest in their children's homework or take the time to attend school activities, such as parent-teacher conferences and open houses, communicates that learning isn't all that important; this is also associated with poorer school performance.[9] Society idealizes athletes and actors but not teachers or scholars. Unfortunately, top athletes and actors can earn more money in a single year than even the best teachers can earn in a lifetime. This sends a message to children and reduces the chances that they will develop a passion for learning. In addition to setting an example by their own behavior, what parents say also counts. When parents have high aspirations for the academic achievement of their children, their children are likely to set high goals and be more successful in school.[10]

Another thing that parents should avoid is providing money, toys, or other types of material rewards for performing well in school. As previously discussed in chapter three, "Building Self-Esteem," material rewards reduce intrinsic motivation, and those who don't inherently enjoy learning are likely to learn less than those who do. However, parents should certainly convey how proud they are when their children excel in learning or learn up to their capacities. For example, they can celebrate a good report card with nonmaterial rewards, such as describing how proud they are or doing something special like going out for a celebration dinner. For children who find learning a real struggle and as a result have a very low level of intrinsic interest in learning, a material incentive system could be implemented in order to encourage learning. Intrinsically motivated learning is best, but extrinsically motivated learning is far better than little or no learning at all. For struggling learners, parents should also offer their support and help, and/or the assistance of a tutor or a learning center.

In addition to being intrinsically motivated to learn, we would also like children to be self-directed when it comes to learning as well as in managing other aspects of their life. In order to accomplish this, parents should encourage their children to manage their own homework and to evaluate their own academic performance. At first, parents can help their children list the homework items that need to be completed and the approximate time each will take. They can also help them develop a priority order for accomplishing the homework tasks. Eventually, children should be able to organize their homework schedule and manage their own time. Parents, of course, should provide assistance if a child is struggling with a particular homework assignment or subject. When a child hands a parent a report card, the parent should refrain from providing feedback until the child has a chance to do so. To help children become self-directed, it is important to let them figure out why they got the grades they did and what if anything they can do to improve their performance.

Since doing well academically is highly correlated with a successful future, it is important for children to have sufficient time to devote to their studies. This means that during the school year, they should not be overburdened with many household responsibilities or employed outside of the home for large amounts of time. Extracurricular activities may also need to be limited. For optimal learning, they will of course need a quiet place to do their homework and to receive proper nutrition and adequate sleep.

Because education level attained and achievement are highly correlated, most parents are determined that their children will attend college. In fact, from the time their children are very young, parents can often be heard making statements that include the words "when you go to college" and rarely be heard making statements that include the words "if you decide to go to college." With this kind of message being repeatedly reinforced, children who decide not to go to college, because of a lack of interest or ability, often feel like failures. This is most unfortunate, since lots of people without a formal college education are happy and successful. Feeling like a failure as an adolescent because of not attending college increases the chances that future achievement will be limited. Therefore, it is important for parents to understand and communicate to their children that education isn't the only path to success.

How does parent involvement in children's education influence academic performance?

Based on the belief that parent involvement enhances children's academic performance, the Parent Teacher Association and the National Coalition for Parental Involvement in Education have set as a primary goal promoting parents' involvement in children's education. Two categories of parent involvement have been identified: school-based involvement and home-based involvement.[10] School-based involvement includes parents making actual contact with the school, by attending school meetings, parent-teacher conferences, and school events as well as volunteering at school. Home-based involvement directly related to school includes assisting children with homework and school projects, talking with children about what is happening at school and their academic progress, and helping children with course selection. Home-based involvement can also include activities that are related to cognitive-intellectual development but not directly related to school. Activities included in this category are reading books with children and taking them to places like museums, historical sites, plays, and the library.

Research has consistently shown a positive correlation between parents' school-based involvement, parents' home based-involvement of the cognitive-intellectual type, and children's academic achievement. However, parents' home-based involvement of the type directly related to school (such as homework assistance) has not consistently been found to positively correlate with children's academic performance. The type of parent involvement appears to be responsible for the inconsistent findings. According to a report in the *Review of Educational Research*, "Parents' involvement may be particularly beneficial for children (especially those who are academically less competent) when it is autonomy supportive, process focused (does the child understand the learning process), characterized by positive affect, or accompanied by positive beliefs. However, parents' involvement may have costs for children (especially those who are less academically competent) if it is controlling, person focused (how well does the child perform), characterized by negative affect, or accompanied by negative beliefs."[11] It appears that the beneficial type of parent involvement enhances children's achievement through both skill and motivational development. Quality parental involvement has also been shown to help children emotionally (e.g., reduce stress and improve self-esteem) and socially (e.g., improve self-control and relationships with peers).[12]

WHY SHOULD PARENTS AVOID PRESSURING THEIR CHILDREN TO BE HIGH ACHIEVERS, ESPECIALLY EARLY ON?

Because parents highly value achievement, many are determined to raise "superkids." In an attempt to do so, some over-program their children, keeping them busy from morning till night with various structured activities and lessons. They firmly believe that the more they can pack into their children's lives in the early years, the more successful they will be throughout life. They often begin by seeking out the best preschools and sometimes place their name on a preschool waiting list even before their child is born. As mentioned in chapter two, "Giving Children the Best Possible Start," David Elkind calls pushing children to learn things that they aren't developmentally ready to learn "miseducation." Doing so is often stressful for the child, lowers self-esteem, and can be counterproductive, since it is often a turnoff to learning. Parents need to be sure that their efforts are primarily motivated by the child's interests and not by their desire to be able to brag to others about their child's advanced abilities. Even when children show considerable interest in structured activities, parents should be sure to build in some downtime for their children to be able to relax and play. According to a report in the journal *Pediatrics*, "Play is essential to development because it contributes to the cognitive, physical, social, and emotional well-being of children and youth. Play also offers an ideal opportunity for parents to engage fully with their children."[13]

WHY IS IT IMPORTANT FOR PARENTS TO PROVIDE POSITIVE REGARD, REGARDLESS OF THE LEVEL OF THEIR CHILDREN'S ACCOMPLISHMENTS?

Children need to know that they are loved regardless of how much they achieve. It is counterproductive and devastating for children to feel that they will only be loved when they do well. When this happens, poor- and average-achieving children will suffer from low self-esteem and be likely to give up trying to achieve because they understand that they will never be good enough. Also, with conditional love, high-achieving children will put tremendous pressure on themselves to be the best in order to get parental approval—and suffer miserably on those occasions when they are not. They may also become driven people, always striving to prove to others (and to themselves) that they are worthy. This may result in their seeking out positions for which they are not well-suited and rising to their level of incompetence. Finally, when parents communicate love and approval only when children achieve, an external locus of control may develop; the children may work hard to achieve in order to please their parents rather than to please themselves. This, of course, runs counter to raising a self-directed child.

SUMMARY

Parents often focus too much on children's accomplishments and not enough on their efforts. Of the three factors that determine success, children can only exert control over effort (they cannot control their genetics or the quality of their instruction/mentoring/parenting). Therefore, it makes sense for parents to focus on how close a child comes to reaching his or her potential, rather than on how well a child does in comparison to other children.

The three most important things that parents can do to help their children become high achievers are to give them the best possible start (which includes good prenatal and early postnatal care, establishing a secure parent-child attachment, and providing a stimulating environment), build their self-esteem, and help them to become self-directed and caring people, in part through the use of an authoritative parenting style. In addition, it is important for parents to be good role models for achievement and minimize inter-parental conflict. Finally, they should provide unconditional positive regard and take steps to avoid the parent-child power struggle that often takes place during the adolescent years, as well as allow their children sufficient time to establish their own identity.

Since success in school and success in life are highly correlated, parents should do all they can to help their children do well academically. This includes being excited about learning, participating in school activities and events, and providing academic support and encouragement at home. Finally, it is important for parents to avoid putting too much pressure on their children to succeed. Parents should always provide unconditional positive regard, and not tie their love and affection to their children's accomplishments.

CHAPTER 8
AVOIDING THE COMMON
MISTAKES PARENTS MAKE

- Parents often lack a set of guiding principles or parenting philosophy. They fail to set goals for their children and to develop plans for accomplishing those goals.
- Parents often fail to do the things necessary for their children to reach their full neurological potential.
- Parents often provide their children with too much negative feedback and not enough positive feedback.
- By both their words and their actions, parents often unintentionally communicate a lack of respect for their children.
- Many parents are so busy taking care of their children and their other responsibilities that they fail to take good care of themselves.
- When it comes to discipline and parenting style, many parents are either too strict or too lenient.
- Many parents pressure their children too much, often wanting the children to accomplish what they were unable to during their own youth.
- Many parents fail to understand that their own behavior is at least as important as the things they say to their children.
- Many parents do too much for their children.

- Many parents give their children too many things.
- Parents often avoid discussing things that make them feel uncomfortable.
- Many parents forget to tell their children that they love them.

PARENTS OFTEN LACK A SET OF GUIDING PRINCIPLES OR PARENTING PHILOSOPHY. THEY FAIL TO SET GOALS FOR THEIR CHILDREN AND TO DEVELOP PLANS FOR ACCOMPLISHING THOSE GOALS.

Well-run organizations set goals and develop plans for accomplishing them. Well-run families should do the same. Parents should have goals in mind for themselves and their children, as well as plans for accomplishing those goals. For example, if parents want to improve their health, purchase a home, or be able to pay for a college education for their children, they should develop plans that will enable them to achieve those goals. While parents can set very specific goals for themselves, it is best if the goals that they set for their children are more general in nature. For example, goals like raising children who excel in sports, music, or science are too narrow, because not all people have those talents or interests, or would be happy following those pursuits. However, more general goals like raising honest, caring, and self-directed children are to be encouraged because almost everyone is capable of acquiring these characteristics and will clearly benefit by doing so.

With goals and a plan, parents are better prepared to handle situations that come up. For example, a parent who places a high priority on their children being kind and considerate is likely to handle name-calling or fighting between siblings very differently than a parent who cares less about kindness and more about turning out children who are tough and can stand up for themselves. If kindness is a top priority, then a plan that involves immediately confronting any mean or aggressive behavior would make sense. If raising tough children is a top priority, then a plan that involves ignoring sibling conflict unless it escalates into something very serious would make sense. Without goals and strategies for accomplishing goals, parents are much more likely to be inconsistent in the way they handle these everyday situations.

PARENTS OFTEN FAIL TO DO THE THINGS NECESSARY FOR THEIR CHILDREN TO REACH THEIR FULL NEUROLOGICAL POTENTIAL.

Without realizing it, the vast majority of parents don't do what is needed for their children's brains to reach full potential. They fail to understand that early in life the brain is extremely susceptible to both positive and negative influences. As a result, they often don't pay enough attention to what their young children are experiencing. They do things, such as exposing them to harmful substances (consuming alcohol during pregnancy or while breastfeeding) or failing to provide a highly stimulating environment to promote maximum brain development.

As mentioned in chapter two, "Giving Children the Best Possible Start," I helped to establish a Montessori preschool. I was also directly involved in the running of the school during its first seven years of operation. During that period of time, I spoke with many parents who were considering enrolling their children. Almost all of them were interested in two things: the hours of operation and the cost. Unfortunately, very few of them inquired about what the children who attended the school actually *did*. They had no idea if the school was providing the type of environment that would stimulate intellectual and emotional development. In fact, the vast majority of parents who decided to enroll their children made that decision before even visiting the school. I suspected that many of those parents missed the opportunity to provide an enriching environment before their children were old enough to enroll in the Montessori preschool, which at that time was three years of age.

It is never too early to provide a stimulating environment for children. There is even evidence that fetuses in the womb learn from the environmental stimulation to which they are exposed. According to a report in the journal *Pediatrics*, "The fetus not only learns the speech characteristics of the mother prenatally, but shortly after birth, infants prefer their mother's voice, a passage recited to them prenatally, and the theme music of a soap opera watched by their mothers during pregnancy."[1] In addition, infants placed on solid foods prefer the taste of flavors that were part of their mother's diet during pregnancy. They were exposed to these flavors by swallowing amniotic fluid.[2]

When my first child was thirty-four days old, I distinctly remember saying to my wife that I had "wasted almost five weeks of time during which I could have been providing a stimulating environment and promoting her brain development." That night following dinner, I decided that I would not waste any more time and began a stimulation "program" that continued for many years. My goal for that first night was to see if I could teach my daughter something. At home, we had a toy akin to a stuffed animal that was just a round face. When the stuffed face was squeezed, it made a very interesting sound that I had previously noticed captured my daughter's attention. Knowing that infants like to look at faces and that this one made an interesting sound when squeezed, I decided to use it as a reward and try to teach her to raise her hands over her head. Placing my daughter on my lap facing me, I put the toy face in front of her and squeezed it whenever she made any arm movements. Using a shaping procedure, I gradually "required" her to move her arms higher and higher before I would bring the face into her view and squeeze it. She seemed to be fascinated by this, and her attention remained focused on the activity for an entire two-hour period, except for about a twenty-minute period of time when my wife was breastfeeding her. By the end of the two hours, my daughter was raising her hands well above her head in order to get me to reward her by bringing the face into her view.

There are virtually an endless number of different types of stimulation that parents can provide. Many, but certainly not all, involve teaching children something new. As mentioned in chapter two, "Giving Children the Best Possible Start," it is important to provide a wide variety of increasingly complex stimulation, as long as a child remains interested. It is fine to challenge young children, but it is important to avoid pressuring them to learn things that they are uninterested in or not developmentally ready to learn.

When my children were about eight and four years old, one type of increasingly complex stimulation I provided was a memory game. I would name a few objects that were located in the room we were in, and they would have to walk or run over and touch them in the order that the items were mentioned. As they got better at the task, I would challenge them by gradually increasing the number of items they would have to sequentially touch. When my younger daughter appeared to be jealous of the larger number of objects that my older daughter was able to remember, I changed the task for my older daughter, requiring her to touch the items in the reverse order that they were mentioned, and thus was able to come close to equaling the number of objects that they each needed to touch. Because developmentally it would have been too difficult for a four-year-old to touch items in reverse order, I didn't ask my younger daughter do so. When either of them appeared to get tired of the game, we of course went on to other activities that interested them.

PARENTS OFTEN PROVIDE THEIR CHILDREN WITH TOO MUCH NEGATIVE FEEDBACK AND NOT ENOUGH POSITIVE FEEDBACK.

These days, most parents are extremely busy and often fail to take the time to catch their children being good. Often children go unnoticed until they engage in a behavior that is unacceptable. As a result, children are less likely to repeat good or desirable behaviors, since that often isn't acknowledged, and more likely to engage in undesirable behaviors, since even negative parental feedback is better than no attention at all. Of course, if a child were to hear mostly negative feedback from parents, self-esteem would be weakened.

If parental feedback were to be directed more at desirable behaviors, children would engage in those behaviors more and not resort to being naughty as a way to gain parental attention. In order to catch children being good, parents merely need to observe what their children are doing and then compliment them by saying things like "Thanks for putting away your toys—it is so much easier to walk through the living room," "I like the way you shared your toys with your friends—I'm sure they will want to come play with you again," or "It was so nice of you to help your brother find his missing shoe—did you see the big smile on his face when you handed it to him?" There is nothing that encourages children more and helps to build their self-esteem than positive feedback from parents.

BY BOTH THEIR WORDS AND THEIR ACTIONS, PARENTS OFTEN UNINTENTIONALLY COMMUNICATE A LACK OF RESPECT FOR THEIR CHILDREN.

When parents are angry and yell at their children or say mean things like "You're a lazy good-for-nothing," they often are aware that they are being disrespectful. However, there are many other ways that parents are disrespectful without even knowing it. When parents say things like "You're too little to do that" or "That's too difficult for you to do," they are communicating that their children are not fully capable individuals. Instead, it would be better for them to say something like "Let's do that together" or "Would you like help with that?" By the same token, when parents say "You won't understand, so there is no use in me trying to explain it to you," they are communicating that their children have limited cognitive ability. Instead, they should provide an explanation at a level appropriate for each child's understanding.

Parents often have an attitude "that _____ is good enough for the kids." When parents cook a meal of high-quality food, such as steak or seafood, and without even asking if the children would like some automatically serve the children hot dogs or hamburgers, they are communicating that cheap and simple food is good enough for their children. When parents decide where the family will go out to dinner or go for vacation without any input from their children, they are providing a message that their children's opinions don't really matter. How would your friends feel if you were eating steak and served them hamburgers, or if you made dinner reservations without consulting them? If parents were to treat their children like they treat their friends, the children would feel much more respected.

Not giving children their full attention, prohibiting them from certain rooms of a house, relegating them to the backseat of the car, or having them share a bedroom much smaller than their parents' and without a connecting bathroom are among the many other ways that parents communicate that children are second-class citizens.

When parents do things for children that the children are capable of doing for themselves, they communicate a lack of confidence. This increases dependency, lowers self-esteem, and deprives children of the satisfaction gained from being able to accomplish things on their own. When children are given the opportunity to prepare a meal, they typically feel a great sense of pride and are much more likely to enjoy the meal, compared to a meal prepared by their parents. When older children are given the opportunity to plan the redecorating of their rooms, they feel that their judgment and taste are respected, and they experience far more enthusiasm and pride than when their parents plan the redecorating.

Demanding immediate compliance is another way that parents communicate a lack of respect. Saying things like "Come here right now; I want to talk to you," or "Clean up your room immediately," or "Stop that this second, dinner is ready" are disrespectful. How would you feel if your friend or spouse said to you any of those things? It is far more respectful to say things like "When you finish what you are doing, I'd like to talk with you," or "Please clean up your room this weekend," or "Please find a stopping point, as dinner will be ready soon."

People shouldn't use physical force to control others, especially others they respect. Pushing, dragging, or spanking children is disrespectful. How would you feel if you did something wrong, such as not arriving on time or losing something, and your spouse or friend decided to teach you a lesson by shoving you around? Clearly that would be disrespectful, and you would most certainly want to distance yourself from anyone who did that to you.

In attempts to control older children, parents are much less likely to use physical force and much more likely to use grounding. However, that too communicates a lack of respect, especially when grounding is used for first-time relatively minor infractions, such as breaking curfew. If you told your spouse that you were going out with your friends and would be home at a certain time but came home late, how would you react if your spouse said you were grounded? You would likely see that as disrespectful and a gross overreaction. Teenagers who are grounded for relatively minor infractions often feel the same. Anyone who feels that they have been treated by a person in authority, such as a parent or a boss, in a disrespectful or unfair manner will likely want to rebel as a way to get back at that person. If parents were to administer a more reasonable and logical consequence for breaking curfew, such as requiring the teen to come home earlier the next time out, the teen would feel more respected and more fairly treated, and would be much less likely to want to rebel. Grounding should be reserved for repeated serious infractions. Parents who treat their children with respect are much more likely to be respectfully treated by their children.

MANY PARENTS ARE SO BUSY TAKING CARE OF THEIR CHILDREN AND THEIR OTHER RESPONSIBILITIES THAT THEY FAIL TO TAKE GOOD CARE OF THEMSELVES.

If parents want their children to take good care of themselves, they must lead by example and be sure to provide good self-care. A life of complete devotion to family and work isn't healthy. Parents who give up everything for the benefit of their children are actually doing themselves and their children a disservice. In order to function well, everyone needs to take some time to unwind and enjoy life. Parents who are always doing things for their children and never have time to do things for themselves get exhausted, lose their enthusiasm, and may become angry and resent their children. When parents' lives are totally focused on children, the children may initially feel like princes or princesses. However, over time they often begin to feel guilty when they start to realize their parents are always sacrificing for them. It isn't good for the family when parents have dwindling energy and enthusiasm, and children have feelings of guilt.

When children see their parents taking some time for themselves, they are much less likely to feel guilty or feel that the world revolves around them, which are both good things. They are also much more likely to have parents who are healthy and not worn down, and who have energy, patience, enthusiasm, and little or no resentment for them. Finally, when they grow up, they will be more likely to take good care of themselves.

WHEN IT COMES TO DISCIPLINE AND PARENTING STYLE, MANY PARENTS ARE EITHER TOO STRICT OR TOO LENIENT.

Many people see today's children as disrespectful and out of control, and believe that they are that way because their parents are far too permissive and let them "get away with murder." Those same people believe that the way to raise well-behaved children is to lay down a set of rules and strictly enforce them. They believe that if they were to give their children even a little slack, they would gradually lose their power and ability to control the children. They are obviously not interested in raising children who are self-directed.

Other parents want very much to be friends with their children, and in order to do so are reluctant to discipline them. They tend to adopt a permissive parenting style where most anything goes. Their children tend to be disrespectful, since few limits have been placed on them, and they have never really learned what is appropriate behavior.

As explained throughout this book, children do best and are most likely to become self-directed and caring people when they are raised by parents who employ an authoritative parenting style. This style is neither strict nor lenient. It is a style in which parents establish rules and expectations that they take the time to explain and allow their children to challenge. Children who are raised using this style feel respected and well cared for. Children who are raised with a strict or authoritarian parenting style may feel cared for but are unlikely to feel respected. Children raised using a lenient or permissive parenting style may feel respected but not well cared for.

MANY PARENTS PRESSURE THEIR CHILDREN TOO MUCH, OFTEN WANTING THE CHILDREN TO ACCOMPLISH WHAT THEY WERE UNABLE TO DURING THEIR OWN YOUTH.

Many parents look back on their lives with regret because they were unable to accomplish certain goals. Perhaps they didn't make the team or become the star of the team, or get the lead role in a play. Perhaps they didn't have the grades to get into a top college, or lacked the opportunity to attend any college. Without realizing it, the goals that they were unable to accomplish are the ones they set for their children. In a way, they are trying to relive their lives though their children. Sometimes parents are fully aware that they are doing this, and sometimes they are at best only vaguely aware.

In order for children to become self-directed, they should be encouraged to explore their own interests and set their own goals. If they are encouraged to do so, they will also be much more content and successful, because they will be pursuing their own passions and not those of their parents or of someone else.

During over four decades in academia, I have advised many unhappy students who were pursuing majors their parents had selected for them. In some cases, their parents had convinced them that a particular major was best, often because of job opportunities; in other cases, their parents had simply refused to pay for their college education unless they chose a certain major. In most cases, these students lacked passion for what they were studying and often earned poor or at best average grades. It often took a year or two for them to convince their parents to allow them to switch majors. When this occurred, in virtually all cases grades immediately improved, and the students became much happier because they were now pursuing something that they felt passionate about.

Of course, not all parents who pressure their children do so because they want to relive their lives through them. Many parents pressure their children because they believe that doing so will help them to become high achievers. They fail to distinguish between encouraging their children and pressuring them. Sometimes without even knowing it, they put so much pressure on their children that their children come to believe that the only thing acceptable is to "be the best." Rather than pressuring children to "be the best," parents should be encouraging children to "do their best," whatever that might be. Many parents have great difficulty accepting the fact that their children may be average—or perhaps even below average in a number of areas. Remember, when it comes to sports, academics, social skills, or anything else, approximately half of all children will be below average and half above average. When parents put excess pressure on children to succeed, the children tend to be miserable. Many become extremely anxious, and others realize that they will never be good enough and just give up, thus failing to reach their full potential.

MANY PARENTS FAIL TO UNDERSTAND THAT THEIR OWN BEHAVIOR IS AT LEAST AS IMPORTANT AS THE THINGS THEY SAY TO THEIR CHILDREN.

Many parents expect their children to do what they say and not what they do. However, children learn from both listening to and observing their parents. Parents who "talk the talk and walk the walk" are much more likely to be successful than parents who do one but not the other. When a parent tells a child about the health risks of smoking but continues to smoke, or warns against overeating but is obese, the message is significantly weakened. When a parent tells children that hitting each other is wrong and then punishes by spanking, the message is greatly weakened. When a parent insists on children doing their homework before they watch TV but tends to procrastinate on getting his/her own work done, the message is far less effective. When a parent requires a child to wear a bicycle helmet but fails to wear one, the child is much less likely to consistently follow the rule. Parents need to understand that they guide their children both by what they say and by what they do. Having words and actions congruent with each other is extremely important. When they are not, if you think about it, the parent is actually breaking his/her own "rule."

The way that parents treat family members, including each other, is observed by the children and forms the foundation upon which children will build their own relationships. If children see constant parent/family conflict, they will likely tolerate a high level of conflict in their own relationships. If children observe respectful treatment between parents and other family members, they will likely form respectful relationships of their own.

MANY PARENTS DO TOO MUCH FOR THEIR CHILDREN.

One of the most common mistakes made by caring and devoted parents is doing things for children that the children are capable of either doing or learning how to do for themselves. Since most parents would like to raise children who become independent and self-sufficient, this is counterproductive. Doing too much often begins early in the children's lives. For example, parents often feed and dress children who are quite capable of mastering those tasks independently. Often this is done because parents want to make things easy for their children. Sometimes this is done because parents are in a hurry, and it is much quicker and simpler for them to do the feeding or dressing, or they may lack the patience to teach their children those skills. While teaching children how to do these things initially takes time, it is time well-spent. Once parents get into the helping habit, it is difficult for them to stop. In my parenting classes, a number of college students have described parents who still insist on doing things for them that they are fully capable of doing. One of the most dramatic examples occurred in a letter from a mother that a student shared with me many years ago. The letter ended with the letters "R.T.U.F." When I asked what that meant, she got an embarrassed look on her face and said "Remember to use floss." Imagine a college junior whose mother is still managing her daughter's personal hygiene! Clearly the young woman was more than capable of doing that. Not surprisingly, this was a young woman who lacked confidence.

Parents who have children with special needs are the most likely to commit this mistake. They often feel sorry for their children because they know that life will be difficult for them. So sometimes, without even really realizing it, they do whatever they can to make life as easy as possible for their child. I first became very aware of this when I was about fifteen years old. At that time I was a junior leader of a Boy Scout troop. A totally blind boy who was about twelve or thirteen years old decided to join our troop. He lived a little over a mile away from where we met, and I was asked to go to his house and escort him to meetings by using public bus transportation. As the bus approached on the first day that he was to attend, I told him it was time to take out the fare, which I distinctly remember was fifteen cents at that time. He reached into his pocket and pulled out a handful of change. Realizing that he might not have experience using public buses, I said to him, "The fare is fifteen cents." I expected him to put all but fifteen cents back in his pocket, but he just stood there holding a handful of change. As the bus was now very close, I quickly took fifteen cents from him and told him to put the rest of the money back in his pocket, which he did. I was initially quite puzzled as to why he had not been able to select a dime and a nickel from the handful of change. However, my puzzlement didn't last very long.

One of the first things that new Boy Scouts were taught back then was how to tie knots using rope. Since I had taught many boys how to do this, I didn't anticipate that teaching a blind boy would be particularly difficult, but it turned out to be virtually impossible in his case. It then occurred to me that he might not have been able to identify fifteen cents or tie knots because of a sensory or motor problem preventing him from using his fingers properly. However, that hypothesis was quickly rejected when one day I visited him at his home and heard him playing the piano. He was a fine pianist, and therefore obviously was able to use his fingers.

The next time I went to pay him a visit, the mystery was solved. I arrived at his home shortly before he did and was talking with his mother on their front porch when the van that took him to and from a school for the blind pulled up. His mother stopped in midsentence, dashed to the van, immediately took his book bag, and said, "The milk is poured and the cookies are on the plate." Clearly this was a mother who felt very sorry for her son, and unfortunately her goal in life was to do what she could to make things as easy as possible for him. It is likely that he couldn't do many things with his hands because he got little practice doing them. I also learned on a subsequent visit that his mother had him very late in life. Being a nurse, his mother explained to me that older women often gave birth to premature babies. She also explained that at the time he was born premature babies were put in incubators and exposed to very high levels of oxygen that actually caused blindness. So she was making life easy for him in part out of guilt for having him late in life and indirectly causing his blindness.

In contrast to the difficulties that are often compounded by overprotective parents, I show a videotape in my parenting classes that dramatically highlights how children with special needs are more likely to reach their full potential when parents take the opposite approach. The tape tells the story of a young woman who, as a result of an accident, had to have both arms amputated at the shoulders when she was about three years old. The tape shows that she is fully capable of doing almost anything that a person with arms is able to do, including driving a car, running a business that involves using a computer keyboard (which see does with her toes), and raising a baby from birth without assistance. In the video, she explains that shortly after her arms were amputated, a therapist told her parents that in order for her to reach her full potential they would have to force themselves to insist on her doing everything, including dressing herself. Following the advice of the therapist was the hardest thing that her parents ever did, but resulted in an amazingly capable armless young woman.

MANY PARENTS GIVE THEIR CHILDREN TOO MANY THINGS.

There are many reasons why parents may feel a need to lavish their children with gifts. Some do so as a way to make up for the scarcity of things that they had while growing up. Others do so out of guilt, perhaps associated with not being available to spend much time with their children. Without realizing it, they may be trying to "buy" their children's love. Parents who overindulge themselves may also feel guilty and find it difficult to say no to their children, since they have difficulty saying no to themselves. They are, of course, poor role models. Others provide an abundance of things in order to try to prove to themselves or to others that they are financially capable and devoted parents. Some do so as a way to try to compensate for a serious illness or significant loss that their children have experienced. Finally, some do so because they believe that providing things is the best way to keep their children happy.

While giving children tons of things initially makes them happy, it creates problems in the long run. Children who have too much often fail to appreciate what they have, and when there is resistance to giving them what they want, they tend to have tantrums. Overindulging parents who don't enforce limits tend to be overprotective, and those who cater to their children's whims are likely to produce children who are spoiled. Spoiled children are self-centered, bossy, demanding, unable to delay gratification and controlling impulses, and lacking in concern for others. They may also feel entitled, and as a result be unwilling to work hard in order to reach their goals.

It is important to note that very young children can't be spoiled. Being highly sensitive and responsive to infants six months of age or younger doesn't lead to spoiling but, as previously discussed, does lead to a secure infant-parent type of attachment. Through this process, children learn that they can trust their parents to meet their needs.

PARENTS OFTEN AVOID DISCUSSING THINGS THAT MAKE THEM FEEL UNCOMFORTABLE.

It is unfortunate that discussions with children about important topics like safe sex, alcohol and drug use/abuse, money, and health concerns are often avoided primarily because they make parents feel uncomfortable. However, topics like these are so important that parents should rise above their uncomfortable feelings and talk with their children about them, or at the very least find someone else who is competent to do so. Having discussions increases the chances that children will be better prepared to deal with these important topics.

The focus here will be on money and health, since safe sex and alcohol and drug use/abuse were topics dealt with in chapter six, "Parenting Adolescents."

Parents are often secretive about money, especially if the family's financial situation is extreme. Parents may not divulge that the family has few financial resources in order to avoid embarrassment, or in order not to worry the children. If there is an abundance of financial resources, parents may be secretive for fear that if they divulge that, it may be difficult to say no to their children's requests, and the children may be spoiled. Parents may also be worried that learning about family wealth may decrease their children's achievement motivation. Remember, parents are role models. If children see their parents working hard to achieve their goals and spend their money wisely, their children are likely to do the same even if the family is wealthy. Whether poor, rich, or somewhere in between, when parents don't discuss finances, they lose an opportunity to educate their children about a very important topic.

Young children who do not realize that their family is poor or has very limited resources are likely to ask for many things that the family can't afford; they'll feel guilty for doing so when they are older and eventually figure out the family's financial situation. They may also be upset that their parents weren't forthcoming and didn't have confidence in their ability to handle a sensitive matter. This last statement is of course also true for children who learn for the first time as adolescents or young adults that their family is wealthy.

Many parents keep secret serious health problems that they or other family members have. This may happen because they are uncomfortable talking about the problems, or because they don't want their children to become upset and worry. When children find out, often as a result of a hospitalization or death, that a family member was struggling with an illness that was kept secret from them, they will likely be upset. They may be angry that their parents didn't have confidence in their ability to deal with the situation. They may also feel that they have missed an opportunity to help out. Since unanticipated deaths are the most difficult to deal with, it is especially important to let children know in advance if someone important in their lives has a life-threatening illness. Doing so will also give the children time to let the sick person know how much they care and say their good-byes if death becomes imminent.

MANY PARENTS FORGET TO TELL THEIR CHILDREN THAT THEY LOVE THEM.

It is important for parents to frequently tell their children that they are loved. This should be communicated unconditionally: the expression of love should not be based on what the child has or has not accomplished. Words of affection and hugs from parents mean a great deal to children. Knowing that your parents love you no matter what helps children feel secure and enables them to get through difficult times. It also helps them to feel worthy, thus building their self-esteem.

Summary

In order to limit mistakes, parents need to pay careful attention to what they are doing, and how their children are behaving. If they are uncomfortable with either, they should act promptly to make a change. Delaying action only makes it more difficult to turn things around.

AFTERWORD

Parenting is a complex job that requires an ever-changing set of skills. Because every child is unique, there is no one approach to parenting that is guaranteed to work with all children. However, employing the principles described in this book will significantly increase the chances of raising a self-directed and caring child.

Giving your child the best possible start in life is the foundation for successful parenting. This ideally should begin with two people who are committed to each other and who are both ready to take on the awesome responsibility that parenting entails. Ideally, serious discussions about what is involved in raising a child should begin before a decision to have a child is made. Discussions of this type will help a couple to determine if they are truly ready to become parents, and they have been shown to improve parental harmony and increase the chances of successful parenting.

Once a decision to become parents has been made or an unplanned pregnancy occurs, the most important thing to focus on is the health of the mother-to-be and the best possible prenatal care. This will help to ensure that a healthy child is born, with a brain that has not been comprised in any way. In advance of the birth of the child, the parents should begin the process of educating themselves about normal child development and parenting techniques. They should also begin to look ahead and explore what child-care options are available.

Once the child is born, it is of utmost importance for parents to be both sensitive and responsive to their infant so that a strong emotional attachment is formed. Children who have formed a secure bond with their parents feel safe and secure, and later in life tend to be more confident and caring. It is also very important for parents to provide a stimulating environment to support the development of the child's brain. Such an environment should include lots of language stimulation, plus exposure to a multitude of other types of stimulation, including music, colors, textures, movement, blocks, puzzles, and games. Brighter children are better able to understand the reasons behind the rules and policies that their parents have put in place and therefore are more likely to be well-behaved and to develop a set of values that will serve them well throughout life.

Parents should also focus on building their child's self-esteem, since that is tied to their child's happiness and success in life. A child who has high self-esteem is also more likely to become a self-directed and caring person. The three most important things that parents can do to foster the development of high self-esteem are to provide positive feedback (catch their child being good), to treat their child with respect, and to express confidence in their child. It is important to continue to focus on these three things throughout a child's life.

There is absolutely no question that an authoritative parenting style works best, especially for parents who want to raise a self-directed and caring child. Parents who employ this style take the time to carefully explain why their rules and guidelines are in place, and prefer to use reason and persuasion—rather than power, threats, and punishments—to gain compliance. They believe the primary goal of discipline is to teach a set of values for their children to live by. They begin very early in their child's life to encourage autonomy and independence, by guiding and stepping aside (unless health or safety issues are at stake). They want to give their child lots of experience managing his/her own life in advance of adolescence, so that their child will be better prepared to make the important and potentially life-altering decisions that all adolescents face. By encouraging autonomy early on, they will also help build their child's self-esteem and reduce the intensity of parent-child power struggles that are so typical of the adolescent years.

Finally, parents always need to keep in mind that the way they live their lives is at least as important as what they communicate to their child. Parents need to lead by example; they need to be good role models at all times. The best way to encourage your child to become a responsible, self-directed, and caring individual is for you to live your life in that manner.

Hopefully, with lots of hard work and a little bit of luck, you will raise a child who will help to make this world a better place. Self-directed and caring people are in the best position to do so.

REFERENCES

Introduction
1. Derek Melleby, "World's Longest Umbilical Cord," *College Transition Initiative* (blog), Center for Parent/Youth Understanding's (CPYU) College Transitions Initiative (CTI), March 31, 2006, http://collegetransitioninitiative. blogspot.com/2006/03/worlds-longest-umbilical-cord. html.
2. University of Michigan, "Empathy: College Students Don't Have as Much as They Used To, Study Finds," *ScienceDaily*, May 29, 2010, http://www.sciencedaily.com/ releases/2010/05/100528081434.htm
3. Ibid.

Chapter 1: Getting Ready to Become a Parent
1. M. S. Schulz, C. P. Cowan and P. A. Cowan, "Promoting Healthy Beginnings: A Randomized Controlled Trial of a Preventive Intervention to Preserve Marital Quality during the Transition to Parenthood," *Journal of Consulting and Clinical Psychology*, 74(1) (2006): 20–31.
2. J. B. Petch, "The Couple CARE for Parents Program: Enhancing Couple Relationships across the Transition to Parenthood" (doctoral dissertation, Griffith University, 2006), http://www98.griffith.edu.au/dspace/ bitstream/10072/26837/1/57952_1.pdf.

3. S. G. O'Leary and H. B. Vidair, "Marital Adjustment, Child-Rearing Disagreements, and Overreactive Parenting: Predicting Child Behavior Problems," *Journal of Family Psychology,* 19(2) (2005): 208–216.

4. L. B. Finer and S. K. Henshaw, "Disparities in Rates of Unintended Pregnancy in the United States, 1994-2001," *Perspectives on Sexual and Reproductive Health,* 38(2) (2006): 90–96.

5. *Expenditures on Children by Families, 2008,* Publication Number 1528-2008 (Alexandria, VA: US Department of Agriculture, 2009), http://www.cnpp.usda.gov/Publications/CRC/crc2008.pdf.

6. C. M. Heinicke, "Determinants of the Transition to Parenting," in *Handbook of Parenting, Vol. 3,* ed. M. H. Bornstein (Mahwah, NJ: Lawrence Erlbaum Associates, 1995).

7. J. M. Twenge, W. K. Campbell and C. A. Foster, "Parenthood and Marital Satisfaction: A Meta-Analytic Review, *Journal of Marriage and Family,* 65(3) (2003): 574–583.

8. E. Lawrence, K. Nylen, and J. Cobb, "Prenatal Expectations and Marital Satisfaction over the Transition to Parenthood," *Journal of Family Psychiatry,* 21(2) (2007): 155–164.

9. C. Rampell, "Money Fights Predict Divorce Rate," *Economix* (blog), *New York Times,* December 7, 2009, http://economix.blogs.nytimes.com/2009/12/07/money-fights-predict-divorce-rates/.

10. E. Galinsky, *Between Generations: The Six Stages of Parenthood* (New York: Times Books, 1981).

11. Zobgy International, "Zendoungh.com Survey Finds Nearly One in Five Americans Avoid Discussing Finances Before Marriage," TransUnion, May 5, 2010, http://www.easyir.com/easyir/customrel.do?easyirid=DC2167C025A9EA04&version=live&prid=616656&releasejsp=custom_144.

12. Bureau of Labor Statistics, "Employment Characteristics of Families Summary," news release, May 27, 2010, http://www.bls.gov/news.release/famee.nr0.htm.

13. "Charts for the American Time Use Survey," Bureau of Labor

Statistics, last modified January 19, 2011, http://www.bls.gov/tus/charts/.

Chapter 2: Giving Children the Best Possible Start
1. *Eating Disorders and Pregnancy: Some Facts about the Risks* (Seattle, WA: National Eating Disorders Center, 2005), http://www.nationaleatingdisorders.org/nedaDir/files/documents/handouts/Pregnant.pdf.
2. M. Richards, R. Hardy, D. Kuh, and E. J. Wadsworth, "Birth Weight and Cognitive Function in the British 1946 Birth Cohort: Longitudinal Population Based Study," *British Medical Journal,* 322 (2001): 199–203.
3. M. Hack, D. J. Flannery, M. Schluchter, L. Cartar, E. Borawski, and N. Klein, "Outcomes in Young Adulthood for Very-Low-Birth-Weight Infants," *The New England Journal of Medicine,* 346(3) (2002): 149–157.
4. M. K. Georgieff, "Nutrition and the Developing Brain: Nutrient Priorities and Measurement," *American Journal of Clinical Nutrition,* 85(2) (2007): 614S–620S.
5. J. Liu, A. Raine, P. H. Venables, C. Dalais, and S. A. Mednick, "Malnutrition at Age 3 Years and Lower Cognitive Ability at Age 11 Years," *Archives of Pediatric Adolescent Medicine,* 157 (2003): 593–600.
6. N. J. Thompson, "Fetal Nutrition and Adult Hypertension, Diabetes, Obesity, and Coronary Artery Disease," *Neonatal Network,* 26(4) (2007): 235–240, http://neonatalnetwork.metapress.com/content/457544g01w763361/.
7. "What Is Spina Bifida?" Association for Spina Bifida and Hydrocephalus, last modified March 2011, http://www.asbah.org/Spina_Bifida/informationsheets/whatisspinabifida.htm.
8. March of Dimes (2010). "Vitamins and Minerals During Pregnancy," March of Dimes, last updated March 2009, http://www.marchofdimes.com/pnhec/159_514.asp.
9. M. K. Georgieff, "Nutrition and the Developing Brain: Nutrient Priorities and Measurement," *American Journal of Clinical Nutrition,* 85(2) (2007): 614S–620S.

10. "Fetal Alcohol Syndrome," Mayo Clinic, last updated May 22, 2009, http://www.mayoclinic.com/health/fetal-alcohol-syndrome/DS00184.

11. B. N. Bailey, V. Delaney-Black, C. Y. Covington, J. Ager, J. Janisse, J. H. Hannigan, and R. J. Solol, "Prenatal Exposure to Binge Drinking and Cognitive and Behavioral Outcomes at Age 7 Years," *American Journal of Obstetrics and Gynecology*, 191(3) (2004): 1037–1043.

12. K. C. Sterling, "Fetal Alcohol Syndrome," in *Disorders of Development and Learning*, ed. M. L. Wolraich (Hamilton Ontario: BC Decker, Inc., 2003).

13. Ibid.

14. B. N. Bailey, V. Delaney-Black, C. Y. Covington, J. Ager, J. Janisse, J. H. Hannigan, and R. J. Solol, "Prenatal Exposure to Binge Drinking and Cognitive and Behavioral Outcomes at Age 7 Years," *American Journal of Obstetrics and Gynecology*, 191(3) (2004): 1037–1043.

15. The American Academy of Pediatricians, "Policy Statement: Breastfeeding and the Use of Human Milk. *Pediatrics*, 115(2) (2005): 496–506. http://aappolicy.aappublications.org/cgi/content/full/pediatrics;115/2/496.

16. Ibid.

17. M. S. Kramer, F. Aboud, E. Mironova, et al, "Breast Feeding and Child Cognitive Development: New Evidence from a Large Randomized Trial," *Archives of General Psychiatry*, 65(5) (2008): 578–584.

18. P. J. Quinn, M. O'Callaghan, Q. Williams, J. M. Nahman, M. J. Andersen, and W. Bor, "The Effect of Breastfeeding at 5 Years: A Cohort Study," *Journal of Paediatrics and Child Health*, 37(5) (2001): 465–469.

19. P. Hoddinott, D. Tappin, C. Wright, "Breast Feeding," *British Medical Journal*, 336 (2008): 881-887. http://mypimd.ncl.ac.uk/PIMDDev/pimd-home/specialty-training-1/specialty-schools/school-of-paediatrics/core-training-days/breast%20feeding%20bmj%20review.pdf

20. J. A. Mennella and C. J. Gerrish, "Effects of Exposure to Alcohol in Mother's Milk on Infant Sleep," *Pediatrics*,

101(5) (1998): 1–5, http://pediatrics.aappublications.org/cgi/reprint/101/5/e2.

21. J. Mennella, "Alcohol's Effect on Lactation," *Alcohol Research and Health,* 25(3) (2001): 230–234.

22. W. J. Rogan and J. H. Ware, "Exposure to Lead in Children: How Low is Low Enough?" *New England Journal of Medicine,* 348 (2003): 1515–1516.

23. C. Cole and A. Winsler, "Protecting Children from Exposure to Lead: Old Problem, New Data, and New Policy Needs," *Social Policy Report,* 24(1) (2010): 1–19.

24. V. Jaddoe, B. O. Verburg, M. de Ridder, A. Hofman, J. P. Mackenbach, H. A. Moll, E. Steegers, and C. Witteman, "Maternal Smoking and Fetal Growth Characteristics in Different Periods of Pregnancy, *American Journal of Epidemiology,* 165(10) (2007): 1207–1215.

25. J. R. DiFranza, A. Aligne, and M. Weitzman, "Prenatal and Postnatal Environmental Tobacco Smoke Exposure and Children's Health," *Pediatrics,* 113(4) (2004): 1007-1015, http://pediatrics.aappublications.org/cgi/content/full/113/4/S1/1007.

26. Ibid.

27. P. S. Lizard, M. K. O'Rourke, and R. J. Morris, "The Effects of Organophosphate Pesticide Exposure on Hispanic Children's Cognitive and Behavioral Functioning," *Journal of Pediatric Psychology,* 33(1) (2008): 91–101.

28. W. J. Crinnion, "Maternal Levels of Xenobiotics That Affect Fetal Development and Childhood Health," *Alternative Medicine Review,* 14(3) (2009): 212–222.

29. M. F. Bouchard, D. C. Bellinger, R. O. Wright, and M. G. Weisskoff, "Attention-Deficit/Hyperactivity Disorder and Urinary Metabolities of Organophosphate Pesticides," *Pediatrics,* 125(6) (2010): e1270–e1277, http://pediatrics.aappublications.org/cgi/content/full/125/6/e1270.

30. X. Weng, R. Odouli, and L. D-K, "Maternal Caffeine Consumption during Pregnancy and the Risk of Miscarriage: A Prospective Cohort Study," *American Journal of Obstetrics*

and Gynecology, 198(3) (2008): 279.e1–e8, http://studentweb. cencol.ca/tburden/caffeine_miscarriage_study_final.pdf.

31. American Dietetic Association, "Caffeine Conundrum: Can Coffee Be Part of a Healthy Pregnancy," press release, May 29, 2009, http://www.eatright.org/Media/content. aspx?id=1247&terms=caffeine.

32. M. R. Rosenzweig and E. L. Bennett, "Psychobiology of Plasticity: Effects of Training and Experience on Brain and Behavior," *Behavioral Brain Research,* 78 (1996): 57–65.

33. C. M. Diamond, "Response of the Brain to Enrichment," Anais da Academia Brasileira de Ciências, 73 (2001): 211–220, http://www.scielo.br/scielo.php?pid=S0001-37652001000200006&script=sci_arttext&tlng=en.

34. R. Feldman, A. I. Eidelman, L. Sirota, and A. Weller, "Comparison of Skin-to-Skin (Kangaroo) and Traditional Care: Parenting Outcomes and Preterm Infant Development," *Pediatrics,* 110(1) (2002): 16–26, http:// pediatrics.aappublications.org/cgi/content/full/110/1/16?m axtoshow=&hits=10&RESULTFORMAT=&fulltext=kan garoo+mother+care&searchid=1&FIRSTINDEX=0&sort spec=relevance&resourcetype=HWCIT.

35. A. Guzzetta, S. Baldini, A. Bancale, et al, "Massage Accelerates Brain Development and the Maturation of Visual Function, *Journal of Neuroscience,* 29 (2009): 6042-6051.

36. H. T. Chugani, M. E. Behen, O. Muzik, C. Juhasz, and N. F. Chugani, "Local Brain Functional Activity Following Early Deprivation: A Study of Postinstitutionalized Romanian Orphans," *Neruoimage,* 14(6) (2001): 1290–1301.

37. T. J. Eluvathingal, H. T. Chugani, M. E. Behen, C. Juhasz, O. Muzik, M. Maqboll, D. C. Chugani, and M. Makki, "Abnormal Brain Connectivity in Children after Early Severe Socioemotional Deprivation: A Diffusion Tensor Imaging Study," *Pediatrics,* 117(6) (2006): 2093–2100, http://pediatrics.aappublications.org/cgi/content/full/117/6/2093.

38. US Department of Health and Human Services, Administration for Children and Families, "Head Start Impact Study, Final Report," (Washington, DC: 2010), http://eric.ed.gov/ERICDocs/data/ericdocs2sql/content_storage_01/0000019b/80/46/87/2e.pdf.

39. K. Burger, "How Does Early Childhood Care and Education Affect Cognitive Development? An International Review of the Effects of Early Interventions for Children from Different Social Backgrounds," *Early Childhood Research Quarterly*, 25(2) (2010): 140–165.

40. D. L. Vandell, J. Belsky, M. Burchinal, L. Steinberg, N. Vandergrift, and NICHD Early Child Care Research Network, "Do Effects of Early Child Care Extend to Age 15 Years? Results from the NICHD Study of Early Child Care and Youth Development," *Child Development*, 81(3) (2010): 737–756.

41. M. Senechal, and J. LeFevre, "Parental Involvement in the Development of Children's Reading Skill: A Five-Year Longitudinal Study," *Child Development*, 73(2) (2002): 445–460.

42. K. L. Hyde, J. Lerch, A. Norton, M. Forgeard, E. Winner, A. C. Evans, and G. Schlaug, "Musical Training Shapes Structural Brain Development," *The Journal of Neuroscience*, 29(10) (2009): 3019–3025.

43. K. R. Ginsburg, "The Importance of Play in Promoting Healthy Child Development and Maintain Strong Parent-Child Bonds," *Pediatrics*, 119(1) (2007): 182–191, http://www.aap.org/pressroom/playFINAL.pdf.

44. C. H. Hillman, K. I. Erickson, and A. Kramer, "Be Smart Exercise Your Heart: Exercise Effect on Brain and Cognition," *Nature Reviews Neuroscience*, 9(1) (2008): 58–65.

45. J. Lojovich, "The Relationship between Aerobic Exercise and Cognition: Is Movement Medicinal?" *Journal of Head Trauma Rehabilitation*, 25(3) (2008): 184–192.

46. W. Bruno, R. Galani, C. Kelche, and M. R. Rosenzweig, "Recovery from Brain Injury in Animals: Relative Efficacy

of Environmental Enrichment, Physical Exercise or Formal Training," *Progress in Neurobiology,* 72 (1990–2002): 167–182.

47. Y. Stern, *Cognitive Reserve*, (New York: Taylor & Francis, 2007).

48. D. Elkind, *Miseducation*, (New York: Alfred A. Knopf, Inc., 1987), Chapter 1.

49. M. D. Ainsworth, M. Blehar, E. Waters, and S. Wall, *Patterns of Attachment: A Psychological Study of the Strange Situation* (Hillsdale, NJ: Lawrence Erlbaum Associates, 1978).

50. M. Main and J. Solomon, "Discovery of an Insecure Disorganized/Disoriented Attachment Pattern: Procedures, Findings and Implication for Classification of Behavior," in *Affective Development in Infancy*, M. W. Yogman and T. B. Brazelton, (Norwood, NY: Ablex, 1986).

51. L. Matas, A. Arend, and L. A. Sroufe, "Continuity of Adaptation in the Second Year: The Relationship between Quality of Attachment and Later Competence," *Child Development,* 49(3) (1978): 547–556.

52. J. Cassidy, "Child-Mother Attachment and the Self in Six-Year-Olds, *Child Development,* 59(1) (1988): 121–134.

53. E. Moss and D. St-Laurent, "Attachment at School Age and Academic Performance," *Development Psychology,* 37(6) (2001): 863–874.

54. R. F. Marcus and J. Sanders-Reio, "The Influence of Attachment on School Completion," *School Psychology Quarterly,* 16(4) (2001): 427–444.

55. K. Hennighausen and K. Lyons-Ruth, "Disorganization of Attachment Strategies in Infancy and Childhood," *Encyclopedia on Early Childhood Development* (Montreal, Quebec: Centre of Excellence for Early Childhood Development, 2010), http://cedje2.dev.absolunet.com/pages/PDF/attachment.pdf#page=11

56. H. Harlow, "The Nature of Love," *American Psychologist,* 13 (1958): 673–685.

57. H. Harlow and C. Suomi, "The Nature of Love: Simplified," *American Psychologist,* 25(2) (1970): 161–168.

58. University of Rochester Medical Center, "Nearly One-Third of US parents Don't Know What to Expect of Infants, *ScienceDaily,* May 4, 2008, http://www.sciencedaily.com / releases/2008/05/080504095631.htm.

59. M. Pinsker and K. Geoffroy, "A Comparison of Parent Effectiveness Training and Behavior Modification Parent Training," *Family Relations,* 30(1) (1981): 61–68.

60. M. S. Dias, K. Smith, K. DeGuehery, P. Mazur, V. Li, and M. L. Shaffer, "Preventing Abusive Head Trauma among Infants and Young Children: A Hospital-Based Parent Education Program, *Pediatrics,* 115(4) (2005): e470-e477, http://pediatrics.aappublications.org/cgi/content/full/115/4/e470.

61. "Who's Minding the Kids? Child Care Arrangements" US Census Bureau, Spring 2005, http://www.census.gov/population/www/socdemo/child/ppl-2005.html.

62. S. W. Helburn, "Cost, Quality, and Child Outcomes in Child Care Centers Public Report, *University of Colorado-Denver, Economics Department* (1995), http://eric.ed.gov/ERICDocs/data/ericdocs2sql/content_storage_01/0000019b/80/14/22/e6.pdf.

63. A. Lillard and N. Else-Quest, "The Early Years: Evaluating Montessori Education," *Science,* 313(5795) (2006): 1893–1894.

Chapter 3: Building Self-Esteem

1. B. W. Pelham and W. B. Swann, "From Self-Conceptions to Self-Worth: On the Sources and Structure of Global Self-Esteem," *Journal of Personality and Social Psychology,* 57(4) (1989): 672–680.

2. G. P. Hickman, S. Gartholomae, and P. C. McKenry, "Influence of Parenting Styles on the Adjustment and Academic Achievement of Traditional College Freshmen," *Journal of College Student Development,* 41(1) (2000): 41-54.

3. K. Heinonen, K. Raikkonen, and L. Keltikangas-Jarvinen, "Self-Esteem in Early and Late Adolescence Predicts Dispositional Optimism-Pessimism in Adulthood: A 21-Year Longitudinal Study," *Personality and Individual Differences*, 39(3) (2005): 511–521.

4. K. H. Trzesniewski, M. B. Donnellan, T. E. Moffitt, R. W. Robins, R. Poulton, and A. Caspi, "Low Self-Esteem during Adolescence Predicts Poor Health, Criminal Behavior, and Limited Economic Prospects during Adulthood," *Developmental Psychology*, 42(2) (2006): 381–390.

5. L. G. Wild, A. J. Flisher, A. Bhana, and C. Lombard, "Association among Adolescent Risk Behaviours and Self-Esteem in Six Domains," *Journal of Child Psychology and Psychiatry*, 45(8) (2004): 1454–1467.

6. Ibid.

7. A. H. Maslow, "A Theory of Human Motivation," *Psychological Review*, 50(4) (1943): 370–390.

8. A. Faber and E. Mazlish, *Liberated Parents Liberated Children: Your Guide to a Happier Family*, (New York: Avon Books, 1974).

9. Ibid.

10. W. T. Chan and A. Koo, "Parenting Style and Youth Outcomes in the UK," *European Sociological Review*, Advance Access published on March 7, 2010, doi:10.1093/esr/jcq013.

11. C. Rogers, "A Theory of Therapy, Personality and Interpersonal Relationships as Developed in the Client-Centered Framework," in *Psychology: A Study of a Science, Vol. 3*, ed. S. Koch (New York: McGraw Hill, 1959).

12. A. H. Maslow, "A Theory of Human Motivation," *Psychological Review*, 50(4) (1943): 370–390.

Chapter 4: Discipline and Parenting Styles

1. A. Straus and J. A. Steward, "Corporal Punishment by American Parents: National Data on Prevalence, Chronicity, Severity, and Duration, in Relation to Child and Family

Characteristics," *Clinical Child and Family Psychology Review,* 2(2) (1999): 5–70.

2. N. Malamuth, "Aggression Against Women: Cultural and Individual Causes." in *Pornography and Sexual Aggression,* ed. N. Malamuth and E. Donnerstein (New York: Academic Press, 1984).

3. D. Baurind, "Effects of Authoritative Parental Control on Child Behavior," *Child Development,* 37(4) (1966): 887–907.

4. D. Baurind, "Child Care Practices Anteceding Three Patterns of Preschool Behavior," *Genetic Psychology Monographs,* 75(1) (1967): 43–88.

5. D. Baurind, "Current Patterns of Parental Authority," *Developmental Psychology Monographs,* 4(1) (1971): 1–103.

6. E. E. Maccoby and J. A. Martain, "Socialization in the Context of the Family: Parent-Child Interaction," in *Handbook of Child Psychology, Vol. 4,* ed. P. H. Mussen & E. M. Hetherington (New York: Wiley, 1983).

7. M. L. Jaffe, *Understanding Parenting* (Needham Heights, MA: Allyn & Bacon, 1997).

8. G. P. Hickman, S. Gartholomae, and P. C. McKenry, "Influence of Parenting Styles on the Adjustment and Academic Achievement of Traditional College Freshmen," *Journal of College Student Development,* 41(1) (2000): 41–54,

9. D. Baumrind, "Current Patterns of Parental Authority," *Developmental Psychology Monographs,* 4(1) (1971): 1–103.

10. C. Spera, "A Review of the Relationship among Parenting Practices, Parenting Styles, and Adolescent School Achievement," *Educational Psychology Review,* 17(2) (2005): 125–146

11. D. Baurind, "Effects of Authoritative Parental Control on Child Behavior," *Child Development,* 37(4) (1966): 887–907.

12. "The Ethics of American Youth: 2008," Josephson Institute, 2008, http://charactercounts.org/programs/reportcard/2008/index.html.

13. N. Ausable, ed., *A Treasury of Jewish Folklore; Stories, Traditions, Legends, Humor, Wisdom and Folk Songs of the Jewish People* (New York: Crown Publishing Co., 1976).

14. E. L. Deci, R. Koestner, and R. M. Ryan, "A Meta-Analytic Review of Experiments Examining the Effects of Extrinsic Reward on Intrinsic Motivation," *Psychological Bulletin,* 125(6) (1999): 627–668.

15. P. J. Villeneuve, and Y. Mao, "Lifetime Probability of Developing Lung Cancer, by Smoking Status, Canada," *Canadian Journal of Public Health,* 85(6) (1994): 385–388.

16. M. A. Straus, *Beating the Devil Out of Them: Corporal Punishment in American Families and Its Effect on Children* (New York: Wiley, 1994).

17. S. J. Lupien, B. S. McEwen, M. R. Gunnar, and C. Heim, "Effects of Stress throughout the Lifespan on the Brain, Behavior and Cognition," *Nature Reviews Neuroscience,* 1–12 (2009).

18. K. Schrock, "Should Parents Spank Their Kids?" *Scientific American Mind,* January 2010.

19. E. M. Douglas and M. A. Straus, "Assault and Injury of Dating Partners by University Students in 19 Countries and Its Relation to Corporal Punishment Experienced as a Child," *European Journal of Criminology,* 3(3) (2006): 293–318.

20. C. A. Taylor, J. A. Manganello, S. J. Lee, and J. C. Rice, "Mothers' Spanking of 3-Year-Old Children and Subsequent Risk of Children's Aggressive Behavior," *Pediatrics,* April 12, 2010, http://pediatrics.aappublications.org/cgi/content/abstract/peds.2009-2678v1.

21. University of New Hampshire, "Study Shows Link Between Spanking and Physical Abuse," *ScienceDaily,* August 28, 2008, http://www.sciencedaily.com/releases/2008/08/080827210528.htm.

22. M. A. Straus and M. J. Paschall, "Corporal Punishment by Mothers and Development of Children's Cognitive Ability: A Longitudinal Study of Two Nationally Representative Age

Cohorts," *Journal of Aggression Maltreatment and Trauma*, 18(5) (2009): 459–483.

23. M. Knox, "On Hitting Children: A Review of Corporal Punishment in the United States," *Journal of Pediatric Health Care*, 24(2) (2010): 103-107.

24. M. A. Straus, *Beating the Devil Out of Them: Corporal Punishment in American Families and Its Effect on Children* (Lanham, MD: Lexington Books, 1994).

25. K. Schrock, "Should Parents Spank Their Kids? Probably Not, Task Force Concludes," *ScientificAmerican.com News* (blog), *Scientific American*, August 7, 2009, http://www.scientificamerican.com/blog/post.cfm?id=should-parents-spank-their-kids-pro-2009-08-07.

26. D. L. Espelage, K. Bosworth, and T. R. Simon, "Examining the Social Context of Bullying Behaviors in Early Adolescence," *Journal of Counseling and Development*, 78 (2000): 326–333.

Chapter 5: Divorce and Family Configurations

1. "Percentage of Births to Unmarried Women," Child Trends Data Bank, last updated December 2010, http://www.childtrendsdatabank.org/?q=node/196.

2. B. Stevenson and J. Wolfers, "Marriage and Divorce: Changes and Their Driving Forces," *Journal of Economic Perspectives*, 21(2) (2007): 27–52.

3. S. Wallerstein, M. Lewis, and S. Blakeslee, *The Unexpected Legacy of Divorce: A 25 Year Landmark Study*, (New York: Hyperion, 2000).

4. J. B. Kelly, "Children's Adjustment in Conflicted Marriage and Divorce: A Decade Review of Research," *Journal of the American Academy of Child and Adolescent Psychiatry*, 39(8) (2000): 963–973.

5. J. K. Kiecolt-Glaser, L. D. Fisher, P. Ogrocki, J. C. Stout, C. E. Spiecher, and R. Glaser, "Marital, Quality, Marital Disruption, and Immune Function," *Psychosomatic Medicine*, 49 (1987): 13–34.

6. P. R. Amato, "The Impact of Family Formation Change on the Cognitive, Social, and Emotional Well-Being of the Next Generation," *The Future of Children*, 15(2) (2005): 75–96.

7. J. S. Wallerstein and S. Blakeslee, *Second Chances: Men, Women and Children a Decade After Divorce*, (New York: Ticknor & Fields, 1989).

8. R. L. Simons, J. Beaman, R. D. Conger, and W. Chao, "Stress, Support, and Antisocial Behavior Trait as Determinants of Emotional Well-Being and Parenting," *Journal of Marriage and Family*, 55(2) (1993): 385–398.

9. C. E. Cooper, S. S. McLanahan, S. O. Meadows, and J. Brooks-Gunn, "Family Structure Transitions and Maternal Parenting Stress," *Journal of Marriage and Family*, 71(3) (2009): 558–574.

10. E. Thomson, S. S. McLanahan, and R. B. Curtin, "Family Structure, Gender, and Parental Socialization," *Journal of Marriage and Family*, 54(2) (1992): 368–378.

11. J. T. Cookston, "Parental Supervision and Family Structure: Effects on Adolescent Problem Behaviors," *Journal of Divorce and Remarriage*, 32(1/2) (1999): 107–122.

12. S. S. McLanahan and G. D. Sandefur, *Growing Up With a Single Parent: What Hurts, What Helps* (Cambridge, MA: Harvard University Press, 1994).

13. "People in Families by Family Structure, Age, and Sex, Iterated by Income-to-Poverty Ration and Race: 2006," U. S. Census Bureau, last modified August 28, 2007, http://pubdb3.census.gov/macro/032007/pov/new02_100_01.htm.

14. S. Wallerstein, M. Lewis, and S. Blakeslee, *The Unexpected Legacy of Divorce: A 25 Year Landmark Study*, (New York: Hyperion, 2000).

15. J. S. Wallerstein and S. Blakeslee, *Second Chances: Men, Women and Children a Decade After Divorce* (New York: Ticknor & Fields, 1989).

16. S. Halpern-Meeken and L. Tach, "Heterogeneity in Two-Parent Families and Adolescent Well-Being," *Journal of Marriage and Family,* 70(2) (2008): 435-451.

17. E. M. Hetherington and J. Kelly, *For Better or For Worse: Divorce Reconsidered,* (New York: W.W. Norton and Company, 2002).

18. Ibid.

19. J. B. Kelly, "Children's Adjustment in Conflicted Marriage and Divorce: A Decade Review of Research," *Journal of the American Academy of Child and Adolescent Psychiatry,* 39(8) (2000): 963–973.

20. J. S. Wallerstein and S. Blakeslee, *Second Chances: Men, Women and Children a Decade after Divorce* (New York: Ticknor & Fields, 1989).

21. E. Marquardt, *Between Two Worlds: The Inner Lives of Children of Divorce,* (New York: Random House, Inc., 2005).

22. J. S. Wallerstein and S. Blakeslee, *Second Chances: Men, Women and Children a Decade after Divorce* (New York: Ticknor & Fields, 1989).

23. P. R. Amato and A. Booth, "A Prospective Study of Divorce and Parent-Child Relationships," *Journal of Marriage and Family,* 58(2) (1996): 356–365.

24. E. M. Hetherington and J. Kelly, *For Better or For Worse: Divorce Reconsidered* (New York: W.W. Norton and Company, 2002).

25. C. Ahrons, *We're Still Family* (New York: Harper Collins, 2004).

26. B. S. Cains, "Parental Divorce during the College Years," *Psychiatry,* 52 (1989): 135–146.

27. E. Marquardt, *Between Two Worlds: The Inner Lives of Children of Divorce* (New York: Random House, Inc., 2005).

28. E. M. Cummings and P. T. Davies, *Children and Marital Conflict: The Impact of Family Dispute and Resolution.* (New York: Gillford Publication, Inc., 1994).

29. M. El-Sheikh, J. A. Buckhalt, P. S. Keller, E. M. Cummings, and C. Acebo, "Child Emotional Insecurity and Academic Achievement: The Role of Sleep Disruptions," *Journal of Family Psychology,* 21(1) (2007): 29–38.

30. P. R. Amato, L. S. Loomis, and A. Booth, "Parental Divorce, Marital Conflict, and Offspring Well-Being during Early Adulthood," *Social Forces,* 73(3) (1995): 895-915.

31. C. Ahrons, "Family Ties after Divorce: Long-Term Implications for Children," *Family Process,* 46(1) (2007): 53–55.

32. D. R. Morrison, "Parental Conflict and Marital Disruption: Do Children Benefit When High-Conflict Marriages Are Dissolved?" *Journal of Marriage and the Family,* 61(3) (1999): 626–637.

33. R. B. Sears, G. Gates, and W. B. Rubenstein, "Same-Sex couples, and Same-Sex Couples Raising Children in the United States," *The Williams Project on Sexual Orientation Law and Public Policy,* 1–18 (2005).

34. A. P. Romero, A. K. Baumle, and M. V. Badgett, "Census Snapshot," *Williams Institute,* 1–5 (2007), http://www.law.ucla.edu/williamsinstitute/publications/USCensusSnapshot.pdf.

35. E. C. Perrin, "Technical Report: Coparent or Second Parent Adoption by Same-Sex Parents," *Pediatrics,* 109(2) (2002): 341–344, http://pediatrics.aappublications.org/cgi/content/full/109/2/341.

36. J. Wainwright, S. T. Russell, and C. J. Patterson, "Psychosocial Adjustment, School Outcomes, and Romantic Relationships of Adolescents with Same-Sex Parents," *Child Development,* 75(6) (2004): 1886–1898.

37. A. Goldberg, *Lesbian and Gay Parents and Their Children: Research on the Family Life Cycle,* (Washington, DC: American Psychological Association, 2009).

38. "Table C4. Children/1 with Grandparents by Presence of Parents, Sex, Race, and Hispanic Origin/2 for Selected Characteristics: 2009," US Census Bureau, http://www.

census.gov/population/www/socdemo/hh-fam/cps2009.
html.

39. T. Simmons and J. L. Dye, "Grandparents Living with Grandchildren: 2000," *US Census Bureau Brief,* (Washington, DC: US Census Bureau, 2003) http://www.census.gov/prod/2003pubs/c2kbr-31.pdf.

40. B. Hayslip and P. L. Kaminski, "Grandparents Raising Their Grandchildren: A Review of the Literature and Suggestions for Practice," *The Gerontologist,* 45 (2005): 262–269.

41. G. C. Smith and P. A. Palmieri, "Risk of Psychological Difficulties of Children Raised by Custodial Grandparents," *Psychiatric Services,* 58 (2007): 1303–1310.

42. US Census Bureau, "Facts & Figures Special Edition, CB04-FFSE.12," press release, September 20, 2004, http://www.census.gov/PressRelease/www/releases/archives/facts_for_features_special_editions/002683.html.

43. D. Brodzinksy, "Adoptive Parent Preparation Project Phase I: Meeting the Mental Health and Developmental Needs of Adoptive Children," *Evan B. Donaldson Adoption Institute,* 1-18 (2008), http://www.adoptioninstitute.org/publications/2008_02_Parent_Preparation.pdf.

44. US Census Bureau, "Facts & Figures Special Edition, CB04-FFSE.12," press release, September 20, 2004, http://www.census.gov/Press-Release/www/releases/archives/facts_for_features_special_editions/002683.html.

45. E. A. Carlson, "A Prospective Longitudinal Study of Attachment Disorganization/Disorientation," *Child Development,* 69(4) (1998): 1107–1128.

46. K. Lyons-Ruth, L. Alpern, and B. Repacholi, "Disorganized Infant Attachment Classification and Maternal Psychosocial Problems as Predictors of Hostile-Aggressive Behavior in the Preschool Classroom," *Child Development,* 64 (1993): 572–585.

47. P. Leung, S. Erich, H. Kanenberg, "A Comparison of Family Functioning in Gay/lesbian, Heterosexual and Special Needs Adoptions," *Children and Youth Services Review,* 27 (2005): 1031–1044.

48. J. Haugaard, "Is Adoption a Risk Factor for the Development of Adjustment Problems?" *Clinical Psychology Review*, 18(1) (1998): 47–99.

49. M. A. Keyes, A, Sharma, I. J. Elkins, W. G. Iacono, and M. McGue "The Mental Health of US Adolescents Adopted in Infancy," *Archives of Pediatric Adolescent Medicine*, 162(5) (2008): 419–425.

50. A. R. Sharma, M. K. McGue, and P. L. Benson, "The Emotional and Behavioral Adjustment of United States Adopted Adolescents: Part II – Age at Adoption," *Children and Youth Services Review*, 18(1-2) (1996): 101–114.

51. M. A. Keyes, A. Sharma, I. J. Elkins, W. G. Iacono, and M. McGue, "The Mental Health of US Adolescents Adopted in Infancy," *Archives of Pediatric Adolescent Medicine*, 162(5) (2008): 419–425.

52. A. R. Sharma, M. K. McGue, P. L. Benson, "The Emotional and Behavioral Adjustment of United States Adopted Adolescents: Part I – An Overview," *Children and Youth Services Review*, 18(1-2) (1996): 83–100.

53. US Census Bureau, "Facts & Figures Special Edition, CB04-FFSE.12," press release, September 20, 2004, http://www.census.gov/PressRelease/www/releases/archives/facts_for_features_special_editions/002683.html

54. D. Brodzinsky, "Long-Term Outcomes in Adoption," *The Future of Children*, 3(1) (1993): 153–166.

Chapter 6: Parenting Adolescents

1. H. B. Fox, M. A. McManus, and K. N. Arnold, "Significant Multiple Risk Taking Behaviors among U.S. High School Students," *The National Alliance to Advance Adolescent Health*, Fact Sheet No. 8. (2010), http://thenationalalliance.org/jan07/factsheet8.pdf.

2. Centers for Disease Control and Prevention, "Youth Risk Behavior Surveillance—2005, Table 44," *Morbidity and Mortality Weekly Report*, June 9, 2006, http://www.cdc.gov/mmwr/PDF/SS/SS5505.pdf.

3. C. Lescano, B. Vazquez, E. Litvin, and L. Brown, "Condom Use with 'Casual' and 'Main' Partners: What's in a Name?" *Journal of Adolescent Health*, 39(3) (2006): 443.e1-443e7, http://www.region8ipp.com/Docs/Articles/teens_and_condom_use.pdf.

4. S. E. Forhan, S. L. Gottlieb, M. R. Sternberg, F. Xu, S. B. Datta, G. McQuillan, S. M. Berman, and L. E. Markowitz, "Prevalence of Sexually Transmitted Infections among Female Adolescents Aged 14 to 19 in the United States," *Pediatrics*, 124(6) (2009): 1505–1512, http://pediatrics.aappublications.org/cgi/content/full/124/6/1505.

5. K. Kost, S. Henshaw, and L. Carlin, *U.S. Teenage Pregnancies, Births and Abortions: National and State Trends and Trends by Race and Ethnicity* (New York: Guttmacher Institute, 2006), http://guttmacher.org/pubs/2006/09/12/USTPstats.pdf.

6. H. B. Fox, M. A. McManus, and K. N. Arnold, "Significant Multiple Risk Taking Behaviors among U.S. High School Students," *The National Alliance to Advance Adolescent Health*, Fact Sheet No. 8, March 2010, http://thenationalalliance.org/jan07/factsheet8.pdf.

7. B. A. Aarons, S. A. Brown, M. T. Coe, M. G. Myers, A. F. Garland, R. Ezzet-Lofstram, A. L. Hazen, R. L. Hough, "Adolescent Alcohol and Drug Abuse and Health," *Journal of Adolescent Health*, 24 (1999): 412–421.

8. L. D. Johnston, P. M. O'Malley, J. G. Bachman, and J. E. Schulenberg, *Monitoring the Future: National Results of Adolescent Drug Use* (Bethesda, MD: National Institute of Drug Abuse, 2006), http://www.monitoringthefuture.org/pubs/monographs/overview2005.pdf.

9. Ibid.

10. A. V. McCormick, I. M. Cohen, R. R. Corrado, L. Clement, and C. Rice, "Binge Drinking among Post-Secondary Students in British Columbia," British Columbia Center for Social Equality, 2007, http://www.llbc.leg.bc.ca/public/pubdocs/bcdocs/443562/bingedrinkingreport_0.pdf.

11. R. Hingston, T. Heeren, M. Winter, and H. Wechsler, "Magnitude of Alcohol-Related Mortality and Morbidity among U. S. College Students Ages 18-24: Changes from 1998-2001," *Annual Review of Public Health,* 26 (2005): 259–279.

12. Centers for Disease Control and Prevention, "Youth Risk Behavior Surveillance: United States, 2007," *MMWR Surveillance Summaries,* 57(SS-4): 1–131, http://www.mcph.org/Major_Activities/MHPRC/IM/2008/IM608/NEWS_YRBS_2007_Summary.pdf.

13. Committee on Substance Abuse, "Alcohol Use by Youth and Adolescents: A Pediatric Concern," *Pediatrics,* 125(5) (2010): 1078–1087, http://pediatrics.aappublications.org/cgi/content/full/125/5/1078.

14. Ibid.

15. M. D. De Bellis, D. B. Clark, S. R. Beers, P. H. Soloff, A. M. Boring, J. Hall, A. Kersh, and M. S. Keshavan, "Hippocampal Volume in Adolescent-Onset Alcohol Use Disorders," *American Journal of Psychiatry,* 157 (2000): 734–744.

16. "National Survey on Drug Use and Health: National Findings 2008," US Department of Health and Human Services: Substance Abuse and Mental Health Services Administration, last updated September 10, 2009, http://www.oas.samhsa.gov/nsduh/2k8nsduh/2k8Results.cfm.

17. American Academy of Child and Adolescent Psychiatry, "Teens: Alcohol and Other Drugs," *Facts for Families, No. 3,* May 2008, http://www.aacap.org/galleries/FactsForFamilies/03_teens_alcohol_and_other_drugs.pdf.

18. W. Katon, L. Richardson, J. Russo, C. A. McCarty, C. Rockhill, E. McCauley, J. Richards, and D. C. Grossman, "Depressive Symptoms in Adolescence: The Association with Multiple Risk Taking Behaviors," *General Hospital Psychiatry,* 32(3) (2010): 233–239.

19. K. Newman, L. Harrison, C. Dashiff, and S. Davies, "Relationships between Parenting Styles and Risk Taking

Behaviors in Adolescent Health: an Integrative Literature Review," *Latin American Journal of Nursing* 16(1) (2008): 142–150.

20. M. Sheehan, V. Siskind, and C. Schonfeld, "A Longitudinal Study of Adolescent Drink Driving and Other Risk Taking Behaviors: Challenges for the Change Process," CARRS-Q, School of Psychology and Counselling, QUT Carseldine, Queensland, Australia, 2009, http://eprints.qut.edu.au/537/1/Sheehan_risk.pdf.

21. L. G. Wild, A. J. Flisher, A. Bhana, and C. Lombard, "Associations among Adolescent Risk Behaviors and Self-Esteem in Six Domains," *Journal of Child Psychology and Psychiatry,* 45(8) (2004): 1454–1476.

22. W. T. Chan and A. Koo, "Parenting Style and Youth Outcomes in the UK," *European Sociological Review,* Advance Access published on March 7, 2010; doi:10.1093/esr/jcq013.

23. K. Newman, L. Harrison, C. Dashiff, and S. Davies, "Relationships between Parenting Styles and Risk Taking Behaviors in Adolescent Health: an Integrative Literature Review," *Latin American Journal of Nursing* 16(1) (2008), 142–150.

24. M. K. Beckett, M. N. Elliott, S. M. David, E. Kanouse, R. Corona, D. J. Klein, and M. A. Schuster, "Timing of Parent and Child Communication about Sexuality Relative to Children's Sexual Behaviors," *Pediatrics,* 125 (2010): 34–42, http://pediatrics.aappublications.org/cgi/content/abstract/peds.2009-0806v1.

25. K. S. Miller, M. L. Levin, D. J. Whitaker, and X. Xu, "Patterns of Condom Use among Adolescents: The Impact of Mother-Adolescent Communication," *American Journal of Public Health,* 88(10) (1998): 1542–1544.

26. T. Shafii, K. Stovel, R. Davis, and K. Holmes, "Is Condom Use Habit Forming? Condom Use at Sexual Debut and Subsequent Condom Use," *Sexually Transmitted Diseases,* 31(6) (2004): 366–372.

27. R. L. Corey, E. Votruba-Drzal, and H. S. Schindler, "Fathers' and Mothers' Parenting Predicting and Responding to Adolescent Sexual Risk Behaviors," *Child Development,* 80(3) (2009): 808–827.

28. L. B. Finer and S. K. Henshaw, "Disparities in Rates of Unintended Pregnancy in the United States, 1994 and 2001," *Perspectives on Sexual and Reproductive Health,* 38(2) (2006): 90–96.

29. L. D. Johnston, P. M. O'Malley, J. G. Bachman, and J. E. Schulenberg, *Monitoring the Future: National Results of Adolescent Drug Use* (Bethesda, MD: National Institute of Drug Abuse, 2005), http://www.monitoringthefuture.org/pubs/monographs/overview2005.pdf.

30. National Institutes of Health, "Alcohol Related Traffic Deaths," fact sheet, 2006, http://www.nih.gov/about/researchresultsforthepublic/AlcoholRelatedTrafficDeaths.pdf.

31. "Alcohol-Related Traffic Fatalities According to Age Groups, United States, 1982–2004," National Institute on Alcohol and Drug Abuse, last updated November 2006, http://www.niaaa.nih.gov/Resources/DatabaseResources/QuickFacts/TrafficCrashes/crash04.htm.

32. D. Elkind, "Egocentrism in Adolescence," *Child Development,* 38 (1967): 1025–1034.

33. R. Turrisi, J. Jaccard, R. Taki, H. Dunnam, and J. Grimes, "Examination of the Short-Term Efficacy of a Parent Intervention to Reduce College Student Drinking Tendencies," *Psychology of Additive Behaviors,* 15(4) (2001): 366–372.

34. P. Norman, P. Bennett, and H. Lewis, "Understanding Binge Drinking among Young People an Application of the Theory of Planned Behavior, *Health Education Research,* 13(2) (1998): 163–169.

35. M. Warr, "Making Delinquent Friends: Adult Supervision and Children's Affiliations," *Criminology,* 43(1) (2005): 77–106.

36. American Academy of Child and Adolescent Psychiatry, "Teens: Alcohol and Other Drugs, *Facts for Families, No. 3*, May 2008, http://www.aacap.org/galleries/FactsForFamilies/03_teens_alcohol_and_other_drugs.pdf.

37. J. J. Arnett, "Adolescent Storm and Stress, Reconsidered," *The American Psychologist,* 54(5) (1999): 317–326.

38. A. J. Fuligni and J. S. Eccles, "Perceived Parent-Child Relationships and Early Adolescents' Orientation toward Peers," *Developmental Psychology,* 29 (1993): 622–632.

39. C. M. Kalenkoski and S. W. Pabilonia, "Time to Work or Time to Play: The Effect of Student Employment on Homework, Housework, Screen Time, and Sleep," *Bureau of Labor Statistics,* working paper 423, March 2009, http://www.bls.gov/ore/pdf/ec090010.pdf.

40. J. R. Warren, P. C. LePore, and R. D. Mare, "Employment During High School: Consequences for Student's Grades in Academic Courses," *American Educational Research Journal,* 37(4) (2000): 943–969.

41. G. R. Pike, G. D. Kuh, and R. C. Massa-McKinley, "First-Year Students' Employment, Engagement, and Academic Achievement: Untangling the Relationship between Work and Grades," *Journal of Student Affairs Research and Practice,* 45(4) (2008): 560–582.

42. E. Erikson, *Identity: Youth and Crisis,* (New York: Norton and Company, Inc., 1968).

Chapter 7: Fostering Achievement

1. G. P. Hickman, S. Bartholomae, and P. C. McKenry, "Influence of Parenting Styles on the Adjustment and Academic Achievement of Traditional College Freshmen," *Journal of College Student Development,* Jan./Feb 2000, http://findarticles.com/p/articles/mi_qa3752/is_200001/ai_n8892466/pg_2/?tag=content;col1.

2. D. G. Unger, L. M. McLeod, M. B. Brown, and P. A. Tressell, "The Role of Family Support in Interparental

Conflict and Adolescent Academic Achievement," *Journal of Child and Family Studies,* 9(2) (2000): 191–202.

3. S. Ghazarian and C. Buehler, "Interparental Conflict and Academic Achievement: An Examination of Mediating and Moderating Factors, *Journal of Youth and Adolescence,* 39(1) (2010): 23–35.

4. Ibid.

5. D. G. Unger, L. M. McLeod, M. B. Brown, and P. A. Tressell, "The Role of Family Support in Interparental Conflict and Adolescent Academic Achievement," *Journal of Child and Family Studies,* 9(2) (2000): 191–202.

6. S. R. Crissey, "Educational Attainment in the United States: 2007," *U. S. Census Bureau,* P20-560 (2009): 1–14, http://www.census.gov/prod/2009pubs/p20-560.pdf.

7. S. Baum and K. Payea, "The Benefits of Higher Education for Individuals and Society," *The College Board: Trends in Higher Education,* 1–53 (2005), http://www.collegeboard.com/prod_downloads/press/cost04/EducationPays2004.pdf.

8. S. M. Curenton and L. M. Justice, "Children's Preliteracy Skills: Influence of Mothers' Education and Beliefs about Shared-Reading Interactions," *Early Education and Development,* 19(2) (2008): 261–283.

9. C. Sepra, "A Review of the Relationship among Parenting Practices, Parenting Styles, and Adolescent School Achievement, *Educational Psychology Review,* 17(2) (2005): 125–146.

10. Ibid.

11. E. M. Pomerantz, E. A. Moorman, and S. D. Litwack, "The How, Whom, and Why of Parents' Involvement in Children's Academic Lives: More Is Not Always Better," *Review of Educational Research,* 77(3) (2007): 373–411.

12. Ibid.

13. K. R. Ginsburg, "The Importance of Play in Promoting Healthy Child Development and Maintain Strong Parent-Child Bonds," *Pediatrics,* 119(1) (2007): 182–191. http://www.aap.org/pressroom/playFINAL.pdf

Chapter 8: Avoiding the Common Mistakes Parents Make

1. J. A. Mannella, C. P. Jagnow, and G. K. Beauchamp, "Prenatal and Postnatal Flavor Learning by Human Infants," *Pediatrics,* 107(6) (2001), e88. http://pediatrics. aappublications.org/cgi/content/full/107/6/e88
2. Ibid.